# 海外藏中国艺术品
## OVERSEAS CHINESE ART SELECTION

### 绘画卷·元
PAINTINGS · YUAN

本书编写组 编著
Compiled by Editorial Team

郭怀宇 本卷主编
Edited by Guo Huaiyu

NEWSTAR PRESS
新星出版社

图书在版编目（CIP）数据

海外藏中国艺术品.绘画卷.元：汉英对照 / 郭怀宇主编；本书编写组编著. -- 北京：新星出版社，2024.12
　　ISBN 978-7-5133-5441-7

Ⅰ.①海… Ⅱ.①郭… ②本… Ⅲ.①中国画–中国–元代–图录 Ⅳ.① K870.2

中国国家版本馆 CIP 数据核字 (2024) 第 056591 号

## 海外藏中国艺术品 绘画卷·元

本书编写组　编　著
郭　怀　宇　本卷主编

| | | | |
|---|---|---|---|
| **责任编辑** | 李文彧 | **特约编辑** | 丁文文 |
| **英文审校** | 韩　华 | **责任校对** | 刘　义 |
| **装帧设计** | 冷暖儿 | **责任印制** | 李珊珊 |

出 版 人　马汝军
出版发行　新星出版社
　　　　　（北京市西城区车公庄大街丙 3 号楼 8001　100044）
网　　址　www.newstarpress.com
法律顾问　北京市岳成律师事务所
印　　刷　河北尚唐印刷包装有限公司
开　　本　889mm×1194mm　1/16
印　　张　15.75
字　　数　394 千字
版　　次　2024 年 12 月第 1 版　2024 年 12 月第 1 次印刷
书　　号　ISBN 978-7-5133-5441-7
定　　价　348.00 元

版权专有，侵权必究。如有印装错误，请与出版社联系。
总机：010-88310888　　传真：010-65270449　　销售中心：010-88310811

# 出版说明

按中国文物学会统计，鸦片战争以来流失海外的中国文物超过一千万件。这些文物是中国文物重要而特殊的组成部分，除其历史、文化、艺术等方面价值，更因其所凝结的民族情感而备受各界关注。

近年来，中国政府积极推动文物追索，国内外学界也涌现出一批新的研究成果，文物流失研究方兴未艾。但受诸多因素限制，海外文物归国面临着许多实际困难，能追回的仍只是很少一部分。在此情况下，加强中外合作、开展联合研究，通过出版、数字化等方式让更多人有机会了解相关资料和研究成果，成了推动流失文物"活起来"、促进中华文化海外传播的一条可行路径。在国内外专家学者、文博机构等的支持下，新星出版社推出这套《海外藏中国艺术品》，希望能为广大读者及学者提供一套可资观赏、查阅和研究的参考读物。

《海外藏中国艺术品》出版之际，我们尤其希望通过这套书向林树中先生致敬。林树中先生自20世纪80年代起，花费近20年时间，自费走遍40多个国家和地区的200多所博物馆，呕心沥血、锲而不舍，记录了大量海外藏中国文物资料，编纂出版了《海外藏中国历代名画》，成为这一领域具有重大影响力的开创性成果。2013年，新星出版社联手林树中教授共同策划了《海外藏中国艺术品》项目，旨在全面整理他对流失海外的绘画、雕塑、书法、工艺品的丰富记录和研究成果。不幸的是，筹备工作开始不久，林树中教授因病辞世，这给整理与编纂工作带来巨大挑战，出版计划也因此被迫中断。

《海外藏中国艺术品》编纂出版的两大关键因素是专家学者的专业把关和海外藏品的图片授权。在重启并继续推动项目的过程中，我们重新组建了国内外专家组成的编纂团队，英国独角兽公司则协调许多知名博物馆向我们开放图片授权。合法取得文物图片使用授权后，编纂团队对入选文物加以鉴别与甄选，按时代顺序进行分卷、编排，并对文物中英文定名、创作时代、创作者、材质、规格等馆藏信息进行逐一确认。

《海外藏中国艺术品》共计20卷，收录文物2279件，来自海外33家知名博物馆，涵盖了铜器（2册）、陶瓷（3册）、书法（3册）、绘画（11册）和造像（1册）五大门类。

此次出版的《海外藏中国艺术品》因故未能收录金银器、玉器、服饰等艺术门类。我们愿以《海外藏中国艺术品》的出版为契机，努力搭建研究交流和成果出版发布平台，期待与国内外有关各方携手，共同推进流失文物领域相关工作，为中华优秀传统文化传承发展和中华文化国际传播作出新贡献。

囿于出版者水平，书中难免缺漏错讹之处，敬请专家、读者指正。

# Preface

According to statistics from the Chinese Society of Cultural Relics, over ten million Chinese cultural relics have been dispersed overseas since the Opium War in the mid-19th century. They represent an important and unique part of China's cultural heritage. Beyond their historical, cultural, and artistic value, they are also of great interest to all sectors of society due to the national sentiments they embody.

In recent years, the Chinese government has been actively engaging in the recovery of Chinese cultural relics, and domestic and international academia has seen a surge in new research, making the study of the loss of Chinese cultural relics a burgeoning field. However, practical challenges have constrained the repatriation efforts, resulting in the recovery of only a small fraction of these relics. In light of this, it has become a feasible approach to enhance visibility and awareness of these artifacts through strengthened international cooperation, joint research, and the dissemination of materials and findings via publications and digitalization. With the support of domestic and international experts, scholars, cultural institutions, and museums, New Star Press has published the *Overseas Chinese Art Selection* series. This series aims to provide reference materials for readers and scholars to appreciate, consult, and study.

Upon the publication of this series, we would like to take this opportunity to pay tribute to Mr. Lin Shuzhong. Beginning in the 1980s, Lin devoted nearly two decades visiting over 200 museums in more than 40 countries and regions at his own expense. With remarkable dedication and perseverance, he documented a vast amount of information about Chinese cultural relics overseas and compiled and published *Famous Chinese Paintings Abroad*, which has become a groundbreaking work with significant influence in this field. In 2013, New Star Press collaborated with Professor Lin on *Overseas Chinese Art Selection*, aiming to comprehensively organize his extensive records and research on paintings, sculptures, calligraphy, and crafts lost overseas. Tragically, shortly after the preparatory work began, he passed away due to illness, presenting significant challenges to the project's continuation. As a result, the publication plan had to be suspended.

The successful compilation and publication of *Overseas Chinese Art Selection* depended on two critical factors: the professional scrutiny of experts and scholars and the license to use images granted by overseas museums. In the process of restarting the project, we set up a new compilation team composed of local and international experts. UK-based Unicorn Publishing Group LLP coordinated with many renowned overseas museums to secure permissions for image use. After legally obtaining their permissions, the compilation team appraised and selected artifacts, organized them into different categories and in chronological order, and confirmed collection information for each piece, including Chinese and English names, the time of creation, the artist's name, material, specifications, and other relevant information.

*Overseas Chinese Art Selection* consists of 20 volumes, with 2,279 cultural relics from 33 renowned museums overseas, covering five major categories: bronzes (two volumes), ceramics (three volumes), calligraphy (three volumes), paintings (11 volumes), and sculptures (one volume).

Categories such as gold and silver wares, jade wares, and costumes are not included. We hope this publication will help build a platform for research exchanges and publication of research findings. We are looking forward to working together with partners at home and abroad to jointly pursue initiatives related to lost Chinese cultural treasures, and contribute to the inheritance and development of China's excellent traditional culture and a wider knowledge of Chinese culture globally.

Despite our best efforts, errors and inaccuracies may be present due to the limitations of the publisher's expertise. We kindly invite experts and readers to point them out for further improvement.

# 凡例

一、《海外藏中国艺术品》绘画卷收录了宋、元、明、清代共 1178 件画作，每件画作由图片和中英文基本信息两部分组成。

二、本卷中画作依照时代分册：宋代 2 册，元代 1 册，明、清代各 4 册，共计 11 册。

三、本卷中具体画作顺序基本依照画家生卒年先后编排，同时兼顾风格、流派等相关因素。同一画家的画作如有准确年款，则依年款先后编排，无准确年款的画作基本按立轴、手卷、册页、扇面形制依序编排；传为某画家的画作，均编排在该画家画作最后。佚名画作均编排于各时代最后，并依人物、山水、花鸟等门类略作分类。

四、本卷中已有中文定名的画作名称，与官网名称不一致的，均依已有中文定名。

五、本卷中以朝代标明画作的时代信息，其相应的英文表述，统一注明朝代和具体起止时间，如"Ming dynasty (1368—1644)"。部分画作有准确年款，均注明。

六、本卷中画作的材质基本统一为纸本水墨、纸本设色、绢本水墨、绢本设色、绫本水墨、绫本设色六种，对应英文为 ink on paper, ink and color on paper, ink on silk, ink and color on silk, ink on satin, ink and color on satin。将 ink and touches of color on silk；ink, color, gold and silver on silk；ink and color on gold-flecked paper；ink and pale color on paper 等统一为以上相应材质。

七、本卷中画作的尺寸基本为画面尺寸，并注明了画面纵、横尺寸，对应英文为 H、W。

八、本卷充分尊重各海外博物馆的要求，将每幅画作的出处和图片版权信息均详细列出。但因该信息并非对画作本身的描述，故未翻译成中文。其中个别博物馆或美术馆，如大阪市立美术馆，未提供该信息，因此未收录。

# Guide to the Reader

i. The paintings volume of *Overseas Chinese Art Selection* contains 1178 pieces of paintings from the Song (960-1279), Yuan (1271-1368), Ming (1368-1644) and Qing (1644-1911) dynasties. Each piece is accompanied by basic information in Chinese and English.

ii. The paintings are presented chronologically in eleven volumes, of which two volumes are for paintings from Song Dynasty, one volume including those of Yuan Dynasty, four volumes for those of Ming Dynasty and another four for paintings from Qing Dynasty.

iii. The order of the paintings within each dynasty generally follows the period of time when the artists lived, taking the artistic styles, genres, etc. into consideration. Paintings by the same artist are primarily sorted in accordance with the exact chronology information when known; otherwise, they are arranged in accordance with the form of the paintings, namely in the order of handing scroll, handscroll, album leaf, fan paintings. Paintings attributed to an uncertain artist, are placed at the very end of the composer's paintings. Anonymous paintings are sorted at the end of paintings of each dynasty in this volume in accordance with the category of figure, scenery, birds and flowers, etc.

iv. The established Chinese names of those paintings which may be given different names by the official website will be retained in this volume.

v. The era of the paintings is marked by the dynasty in the volume. Both the dynasty and specific starting and ending years of the dynasties are indicated in the English description, such as "Ming Dynasty (1368-1644)". The specific creating time of some paintings is already known, which has been presented clearly.

vi. The materials used in the paintings in this volume are primarily summarized into six types: namely ink on paper, ink and color on paper, ink on silk, ink and color on silk, ink on stain, ink and color on stain. While there are numerous varitions, such as ink and touches of color on silk; ink, color, gold and silver on silk; ink and color on gold-flecked paper; ink and pale color on paper; etc. These have been standardized to the above categories for consistency.

vii. Dimensions in the basic information of this volume primarily represent the size of the painting's image, with vertical measurements denoted by 'H' and horizontal measurements by 'W'.

viii. This volume fully respects the requirements of overseas museums, the credit line and image copyright of paintings provided by the museums have been listed in details. However, since such information is not a description of the paintings themselves, it is presented only in English. Some museums or galleries, such as The Osaka City Museum of Fine Arts, do not provide those information of the paintings when displaying them, therefore such information of some paintings is omitted here.

# 目 录
## CONTENTS

### 元
### (The Yuan Dynasty)

1. 云山图 .................................003
   Mountains in Clouds

2. 梨花图 .................................005
   Pear Blossoms

3. 归去来图 ..............................009
   Ode on Returning Home

4. 人马图 .................................013
   Three Horses and Four Grooms

5. 马图 ....................................014
   Bridled Horse

6. 葡萄垂架图 ...........................015
   Drooping Grapes

7. 维摩不二图 ...........................017
   Vimalakirti and Doctrine of Nonduality

8. 黄楼图 .................................019
   Yellow Pavilion

9. 竹石图 .................................020
   Bamboo and Rocks

10. 清泉乔木图 ..........................021
    Old Trees by Cool Spring

11. 谢幼舆丘壑图 .......................023
    Mind Landscape of Xie Youyu

12. 双松平远图 ..........................027
    Twin Pines, Level Distance

13. 竹石幽兰图 ..........................029
    Bamboo, Rocks and Lonely Orchids

14. 二羊图 ................................033
    Sheep and Goat

15. 九歌图 ................................037
    Nine Songs

16. 江村渔乐图 ..........................044
    River Village: Fisherman's Joy

17. 墨竹图册 .............................045
    Bamboo and Poems

18. 仿李公麟人马图 ....................049
    Horse and Groom After Li Gonglin

19. 溪山渔隐图 ..........................051
    Fishermen–hermits in Stream and Mountain

20. 番骑图 ................................053
    Tartar Horsemen

21. 赵氏三世人马图 ....................055
    Grooms and Horses

22. 仿董源夏山图 .......................058
    Summer Mountains After Dong Yuan

23. 老松图 ................................059
    Crooked Pine

24. 渔父图 ................................060
    Fisherman

25. 古木竹石图 ..........................061
    Bamboo, Old Tree and Rock

26. 草亭诗意图 ..........................063
    Poetic Feeling in Thatched Pavilion

27. 秋林渔隐图 ..........................066
    Recluse Fisherman, Autumn Trees

28. 秋林渔隐图 ..........................067
    Recluse Fishing by Autumn Trees

29. 秋山行旅图 ..........................068
    Travelers in Autumn Mountains

30. 墨梅图 ................................069
    Ink Plum

31. 墨梅图 ................................071
    Fragrant Snow at Broken Bridge

32. 梅月图 ................................072
    Prunus in Moonlight

33. 树石图 ................................073
    Rocks and Trees

| | |
|---|---|
| 34. 王维诗意图 ...... 074<br>Landscape After Poem by Wang Wei | 54. 素庵图 ...... 109<br>Simple Retreat |
| 35. 霜浦归渔图 ...... 075<br>Returning Fishermen | 55. 闭户著书图 ...... 110<br>Writing Books Under Pine Trees |
| 36. 滕王阁图 ...... 077<br>Pavilion of Prince Teng | 56. 丹崖翠壑图 ...... 111<br>Red Cliffs and Green Valleys |
| 37. 古木寒鸦图 ...... 080<br>Crows in Old Trees | 57. 九歌图 ...... 113<br>Nine Songs |
| 38. 溪桥策杖图 ...... 081<br>Ramblers over Winding Stream | 58. 云山图 ...... 117<br>Cloudy Mountains |
| 39. 携琴访友图 ...... 082<br>Carrying Qin on Visit | 59. 风雨归舟图 ...... 120<br>Landscape Ink–play |
| 40. 雪山行旅图 ...... 083<br>Traveling through Snow–covered Mountains | 60. 罗浮山樵图 ...... 121<br>Woodcutter of Mount Luofu |
| 41. 有余闲图 ...... 085<br>Leisure Enough to Spare | 61. 仙山楼阁图 ...... 123<br>Mountains of Immortals |
| 42. 墨竹图 ...... 090<br>Bamboo | 62. 霖雨图 ...... 125<br>Beneficent Rain |
| 43. 仿文同墨竹图 ...... 091<br>Bamboo After Wen Tong | 63. 牧牛图 ...... 128<br>Herd Boys and Buffalo in Landscape |
| 44. 秋林野兴图 ...... 092<br>Enjoying Wilderness in Autumn Grove | 64. 绿竹清幽图 ...... 129<br>Pure Serenity of Green Bamboo |
| 45. 江渚风林图 ...... 093<br>Wind Among Trees on Riverbank | 65. 花竹山禽图 ...... 130<br>Bamboo, Sparrows and Camellias |
| 46. 岸南双树图 ...... 094<br>Twin Trees by South Bank | 66. 秋景鹑雀图 ...... 131<br>Quails and Sparrows in Autumn Scene |
| 47. 虞山林壑图 ...... 095<br>Woods and Valleys of Mount Yu | 67. 竹雀图 ...... 132<br>Bamboo and Sparrows |
| 48. 林堂诗思图 ...... 097<br>Poetic Thoughts in Forest Pavilion | 68. 磐石云林图 ...... 133<br>Rocky Landscape with Pines |
| 49. 筼石乔柯图 ...... 098<br>Bamboo, Rock and Tall Tree | 69. 钟馗嫁妹图 ...... 135<br>Demon Queller Zhong Kui Giving His Sister Away in Marriage |
| 50. 墨竹图 ...... 099<br>Branch of Bamboo | 70. 钟馗元夜出游图 ...... 139<br>Lantern Night Excursion of Zhong Kui |
| 51. 九龙山居图 ...... 101<br>River Landscape with Thirteen Inscriptions | 71. 寒山拾得图 ...... 142<br>Hanshan and Shide |
| 52. 夏山隐居图 ...... 106<br>Dwelling in Seclusion in Summer Mountains | 72. 月梅图 ...... 143<br>Plum Blossoms in Moonlight |
| 53. 林麓幽居图 ...... 108<br>Quiet Life in Wooded Glen | 73. 五祖再来图 ...... 144<br>Second Coming of Fifth Patriarch |

| | | | |
|---|---|---|---|
| 74. 寒山拾得图 ......... 145<br>Hanshan and Shide | | 94. 雪景山水图 ......... 173<br>Snowscape | |

74. 寒山拾得图 .................. 145
    Hanshan and Shide

75. 拾得图 .......................... 146
    Shide

76. 达摩渡江图 .................. 147
    Bodhidharma Crossing Yangzi River on Reed

77. 佛渡五比丘图 .............. 149
    Buddha's Convertion of Five Bhiksu

78. 刘晨阮肇入天台山图 ... 153
    Liu Chen and Ruan Zhao Entering Tiantai Mountains

79. 司马才仲梦苏小小图 ... 157
    Sima Caizhong's Dream of Courtesan, Su Xiaoxiao

80. 麻姑献寿图 .................. 158
    Daoist Immortal Magu with Crane and Flower Basket

81. 松鼠栗树图 .................. 159
    Squirrels on Chestnut Tree

82. 丹枫双鸟图 .................. 160
    Two Birds on Red Maple

83. 孔雀芙蓉图 .................. 161
    Peahen and Hibiscus

84. 石竹图 .......................... 162
    Bamboo and Rocks

85. 山水图 .......................... 163
    Bamboo Forest at Night

86. 风竹图 .......................... 164
    Bamboo in Wind

87. 竹石图 .......................... 165
    Bamboo and Rock

88. 水墨花卉图 .................. 167
    Ink Flowers

89. 河蟹图 .......................... 168
    River Crab

90. 萱蝶图 .......................... 169
    Lily and Butterflies

91. 龙松图 .......................... 170
    Dragon Pine

92. 澄溪静樾图 .................. 171
    Quiet River at Foot of Misty Mountains

93. 丹台春晓图 .................. 172
    Spring Dawn over Elixir Terrace

94. 雪景山水图 .................. 173
    Snowscape

95. 竹居图 .......................... 174
    Landscape Under Bamboo

96. 雪中双鹿图 .................. 175
    Stag, Doe and Red Camellias in Snow

97. 华严三圣图 .................. 176
    Sakyamuni Triad: Buddha Attended by Manjusri and Samantabhadra

98. 如来像 .......................... 177
    Buddha

99. 释迦牟尼像 .................. 178
    Sakyamuni Buddha

100. 孔雀明王像 ................ 179
     Mahamayuri Vidyaraja

101. 元照律师大智像 ........ 180
     Portrait of Priest Dazhi Master of Law

102. 罗汉像 ........................ 181
     Arhat

103. 罗汉图一 .................... 182
     Arhats

104. 罗汉图二 .................... 183
     Arhats

105. 罗汉像 ........................ 184
     Arhat

106. 罗汉像 ........................ 185
     Arhat

107. 罗汉像 ........................ 186
     Arhat

108. 罗汉图 ........................ 187
     Arhat

109. 二仙像 ........................ 188
     Daoist Immortals

110. 铁拐李像 .................... 189
     Immortal Li Tieguai

111. 刘海戏蟾图 ................ 190
     Immortal Liu Haichan

112. 达摩苇渡江图 ............ 191
     Bodhidharma Crossing Yangzi on Reed

III

| # | 中文 | 英文 | 页码 |
|---|---|---|---|
| 113. | 寒山拾得图 | Hanshan and Shide | 192 |
| 114. | 元人饮马图 | Horse Stop and Mongolian Horsemen | 193 |
| 115. | 人马图 | Horse and Groom | 194 |
| 116. | 蹴鞠图 | Football Players | 195 |
| 117. | 竹林仕女图 | Lady Among Bamboo and Plum | 196 |
| 118. | 寒山拾得图 | Hanshan and Shide | 197 |
| 119. | 牧羊图 | Sheep and Herd Boy | 198 |
| 120. | 携琴访隐图 | Visiting Recluse with Qin | 199 |
| 121. | 货郎图 | Sweetmeat Vendor and Child | 200 |
| 122. | 宫殿图 | Palace | 201 |
| 123. | 牧牛图 | Oxen | 203 |
| 124. | 山水图 | River Landscape | 205 |
| 125. | 仿范宽山水图 | Landscape After Fan Kuan | 206 |
| 126. | 春山访友图 | Visiting Old Friend in Spring Mountains | 207 |
| 127. | 雪山行旅图 | Travelers in Winter Landscape | 208 |
| 128. | 峭壁松泉图 | Mountain Torrents | 209 |
| 129. | 竹林燕居图 | Retreat in Bamboo Grove | 210 |
| 130. | 柳荫归牧图 | Herd-boys with Water Buffaloes Under Willow Trees | 211 |
| 131. | 秋山萧寺图 | Buddhist Temples amid Autumn Mountains | 213 |
| 132. | 秋林鹤逸图 | Landscape with Pavilions and Cranes | 217 |
| 133. | 古木寒鸦图 | Crows and Bare Trees in Winter | 218 |
| 134. | 秋艳图 | Autumn Splendor | 219 |
| 135. | 牡丹图 | Peonies | 220 |
| 136. | 虫草花卉图 | Melon Flowers and Insects | 221 |
| 137. | 莲花图 | Lotus and Waterbirds | 222 |
| 138. | 粉白荷花图 | Pink and White Lotus | 223 |
| 139. | 花鸟图 | Flowers and Birds | 224 |
| 140. | 长臂猿图 | Gibbon Seated on Branch | 225 |
| 141. | 猿猴图 | Monkey | 226 |
| 142. | 猛禽图 | Hawk on Leafless Branch | 227 |
| 143. | 猎犬图 | Hound Walking | 228 |
| 144. | 龙虎图之虎 | Tiger | 229 |
| 145. | 龙虎图之龙 | Dragon | 230 |
| 146. | 鱼藻图 | Fish Among Water Plants | 231 |
| 147. | 金明池争標图 | Dragon Boat Regatta on Jinming Lake | 233 |
| 148. | 墨龙图 | Dragons and Landscape | 235 |
| 149. | 雪山行旅图 | Mule-train in Snowy Mountains | 236 |
| 150. | 古木竹禽图 | Old Tree Bamboo and Birds | 237 |
| | 版权支持 | Image Contributors | 239 |
| | 编辑、出版人员 | Editorial Staff | 241 |

元

# The Yuan Dynasty

**1. 云山图**

元
（传）何澄
绢本设色
立轴
纵94.6、横39.1厘米
耶鲁大学艺术博物馆

**Mountains in Clouds**

Yuan dynasty (1271–1368)
Attributed to He Cheng
Ink and color on silk
Hanging scroll
H×W：94.6×39.1 cm
The Yale University Art Gallery
Leonard C. Hanna, Jr., Class of 1913, Fund

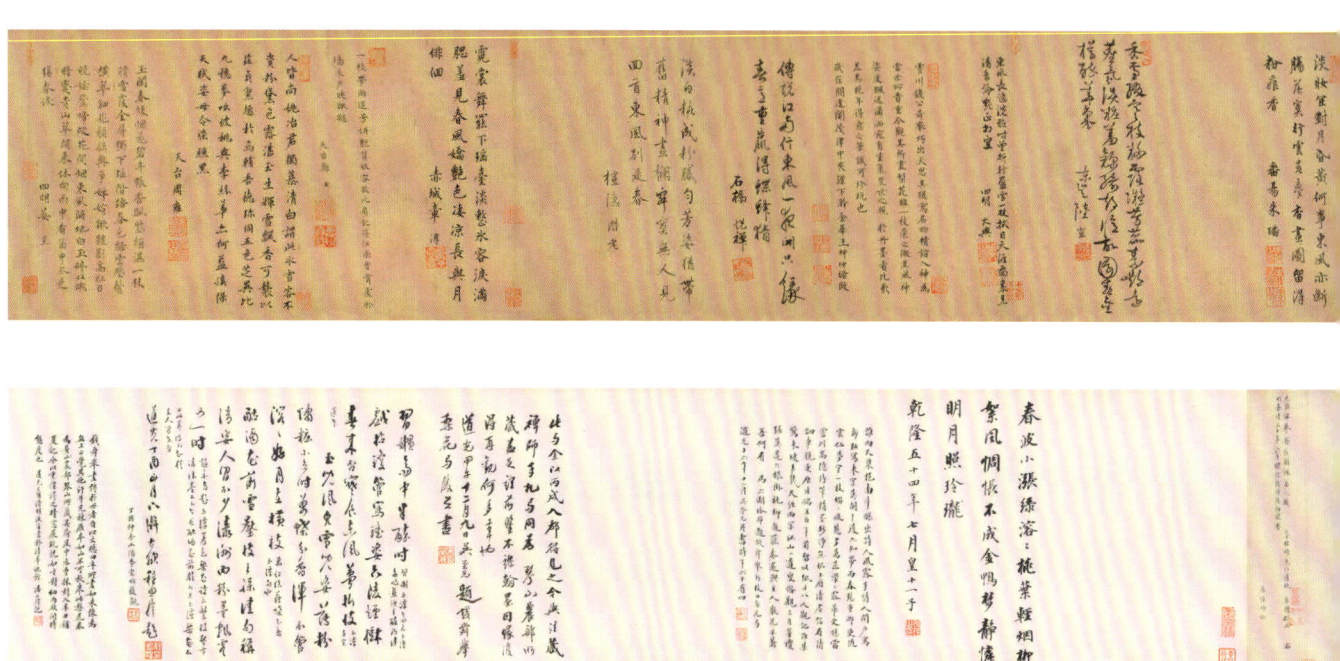

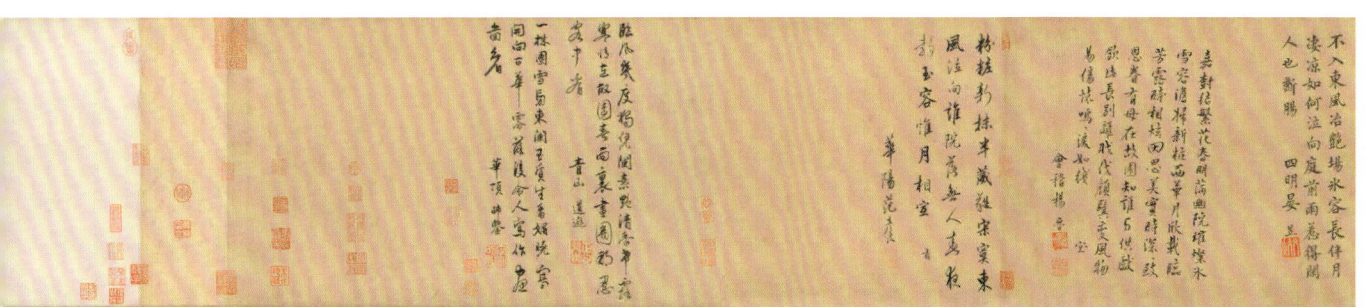

## 2. 梨花图

元
钱选
纸本设色
手卷
纵31.3、横96.2厘米
大都会艺术博物馆

## Pear Blossoms

Yuan dynasty (1271–1368)
Qian Xuan
Ink and color on paper
Handscroll
H×W : 31.3×96.2 cm
The Metropolitan Museum of Art
Purchase, The Dillon Fund Gift, 1977

寂寞闌干淚滿枝洗粧猶帶舊
風姿閉門夜雨空懸思不似金
波欹暗時
雲谿菊錢送春拳

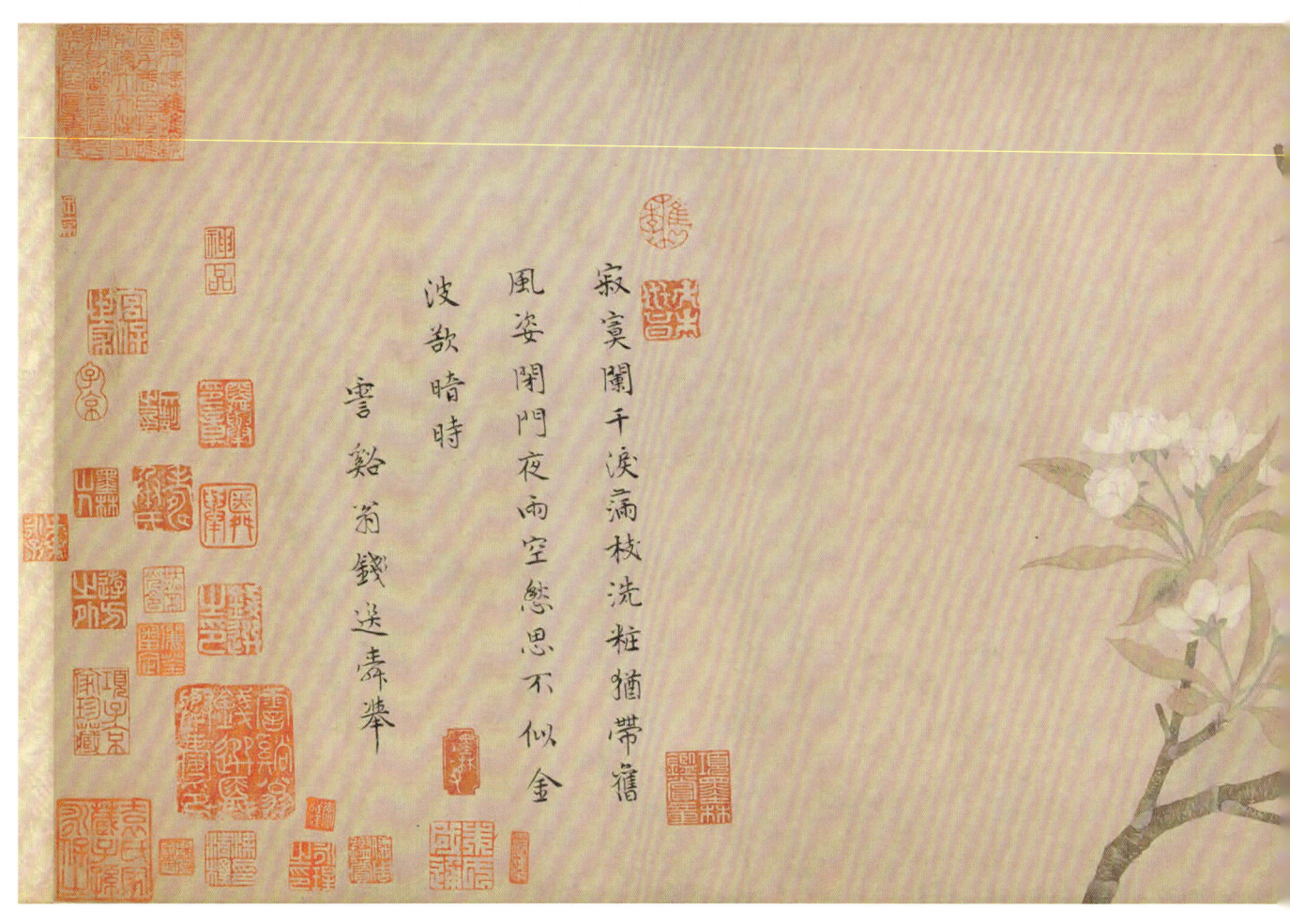

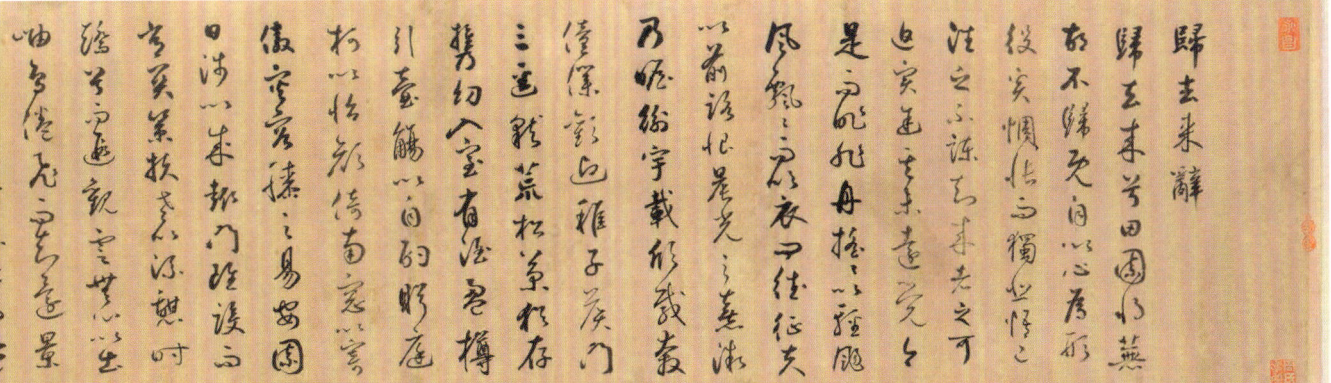

### 3. 归去来图

元明之际
（传）钱选
纸本设色
手卷
纵26、横106.7厘米
大都会艺术博物馆

### Ode on Returning Home

Late Yuan to early Ming dynasty
Attributed to Qian Xuan
Ink and color on paper
Handscroll
H×W : 26×106.7 cm
The Metropolitan Museum of Art
John Stewart Kennedy Fund, 1913

衡明植五柳 東籬采叢菊
長喃有餘清 無奈酒不呈
當世宜沈酣 作邑召侮辱
秉興賦歸歟 千載一醉猶
吳興錢選舜舉

泉明归去赋清解，写傲壶筇谢
云知千载隐名偏称甚画图每写
泛舟时乾隆御题

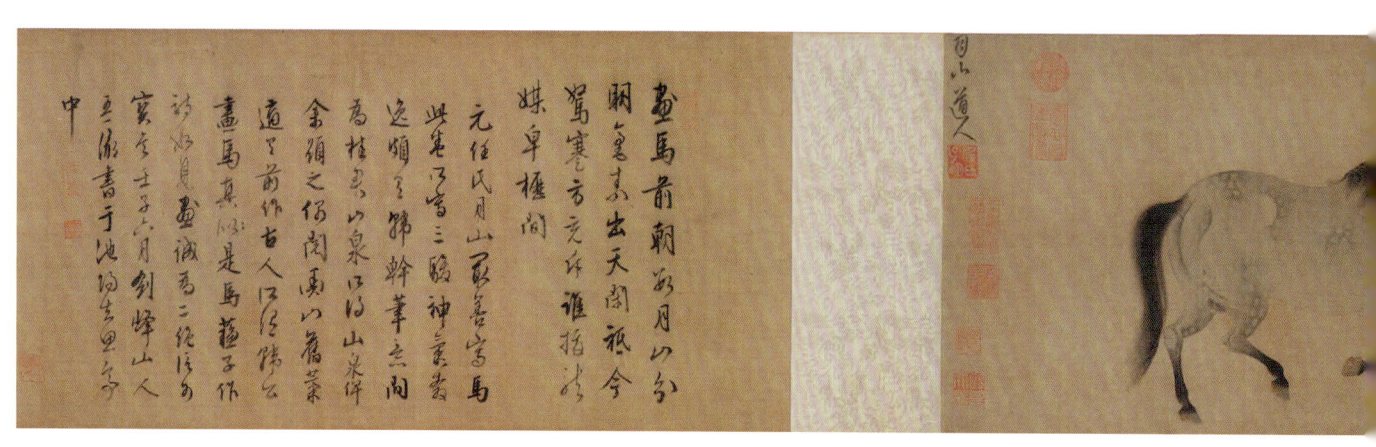

### 4. 人马图

元
任仁发
绢本设色
手卷
纵28.5、横137.5厘米
克利夫兰艺术博物馆

### Three Horses and Four Grooms

Yuan dynasty (1271–1368)
Ren Renfa
Ink and color on silk
Handscroll
H×W : 28.5×137.5 cm
The Cleveland Museum of Art
Leonard C. Hanna, Jr. Fund 1960.181

### 5. 马图

元
（传）任仁发
绢本设色
册页
纵27.94、横28厘米
印第安纳波利斯艺术博物馆

### Bridled Horse

Yuan dynasty (1271–1368)
Attributed to Ren Renfa
Ink and color on silk
Album leaf
H×W : 27.94×28 cm
The Indianapolis Museum of Art
Gift of Mr. and Mrs. James W. Alsdorf

#### 6. 葡萄垂架图

元
（传）任仁发
绢本设色
册页
纵30.3、横47.8厘米
东京国立博物馆

#### Drooping Grapes

Yuan dynasty (1271–1368)
Attributed to Ren Renfa
Ink and color on silk
Album leaf
H×W : 30.3×47.8 cm
The Tokyo National Museum
ColBase（https://colbase.nich.go.jp/collection_items/tnm/TA-122?locale=ja）

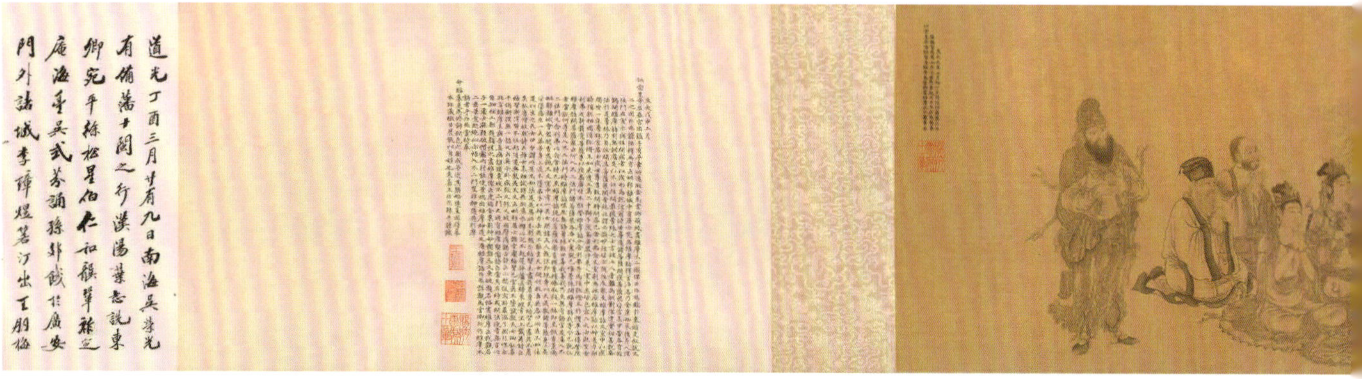

道光丁酉三月廿有九日南海吳荣光
有備藩廿闕之行漢陽葉志詵東
卿究平孫松星伯和顏華
庵海丰吳式芬誦孫非餞於廣安
門外諸城李璋煜著汀出王朋協

### 7. 维摩不二图

元至大元年（公元1308年）
王振鹏
绢本水墨
手卷
纵39.2、横218.3厘米
大都会艺术博物馆

### Vimalakirti and Doctrine of Nonduality

Yuan dynasty (1271–1368), dated 1308
Wang Zhenpeng
Ink on silk
Handscroll
H×W : 39.2×218.3 cm
The Metropolitan Museum of Art
Purchase, The Dillon Fund Gift, 1980

#### 8. 黄楼图

元
夏永
绢本水墨
册页
纵20.6、横26.7厘米
大都会艺术博物馆

#### Yellow Pavilion

Yuan dynasty (1271–1368)
Xia Yong
Ink on silk
Album leaf
H×W : 20.6×26.7 cm
The Metropolitan Museum of Art
Ex coll.: C. C. Wang Family, From the P. Y. and Kinmay
W. Tang Family Collection, Gift of Oscar L. Tang, 1991

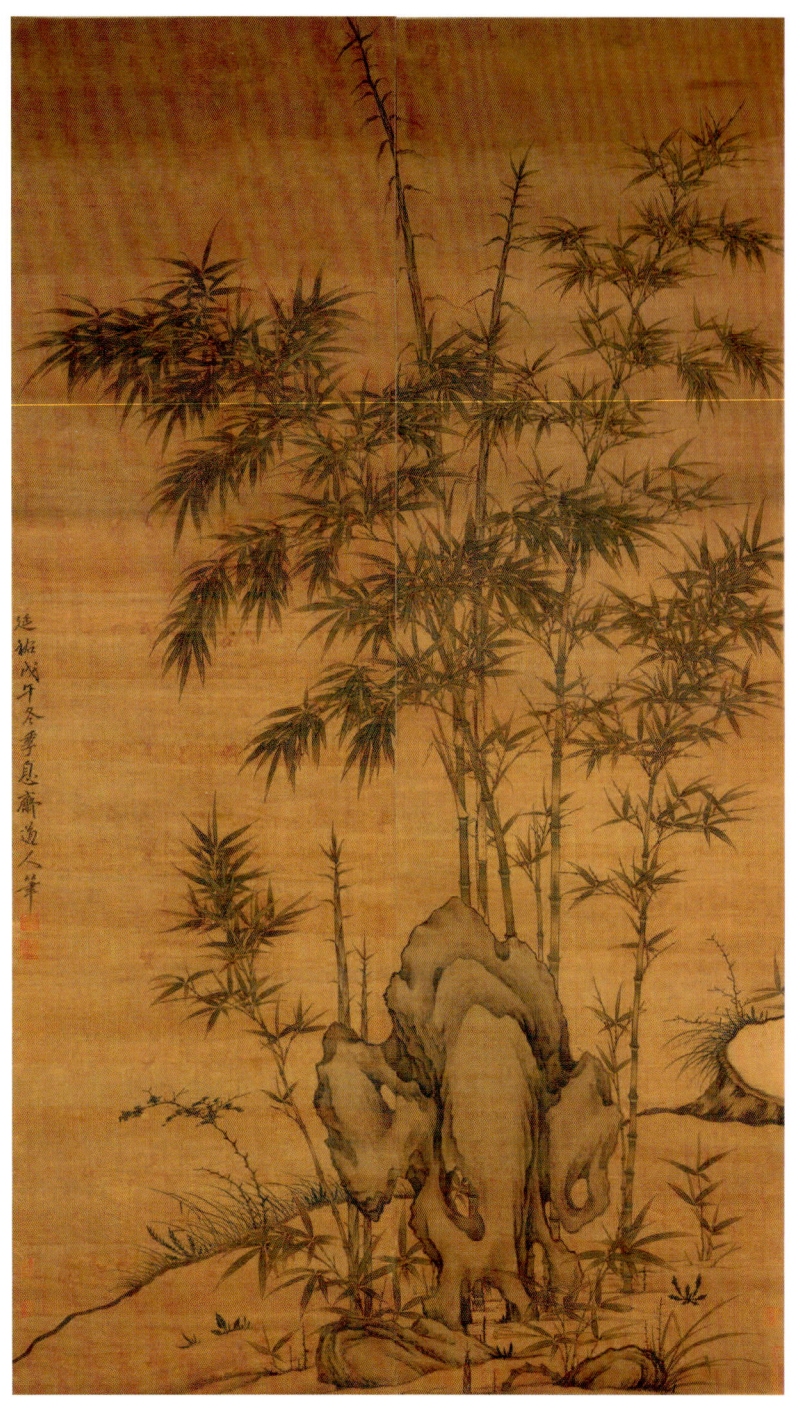

## 9. 竹石图

元延祐五年（1318年）
李衎
绢本设色
立轴
纵189.9、横55.2厘米
大都会艺术博物馆

**Bamboo and Rocks**

Yuan dynasty (1271–1368), dated 1318
Li Kan
Ink and color on silk
Hanging scroll
H×W : 189.9×55.2 cm
The Metropolitan Museum of Art
Ex coll.: C. C. Wang Family, Gift of The Dillon Fund, 1973

#### 10. 清泉乔木图

元
李士行
绢本水墨
立轴
纵165.7、横108.6厘米
克利夫兰艺术博物馆

#### Old Trees by Cool Spring

Yuan dynasty (1271–1368)
Li Shixing
Ink on silk
Hanging scroll
H×W : 165.7×108.6 cm
The Cleveland Museum of Art
Purchase from the J. H. Wade Fund 1970.41

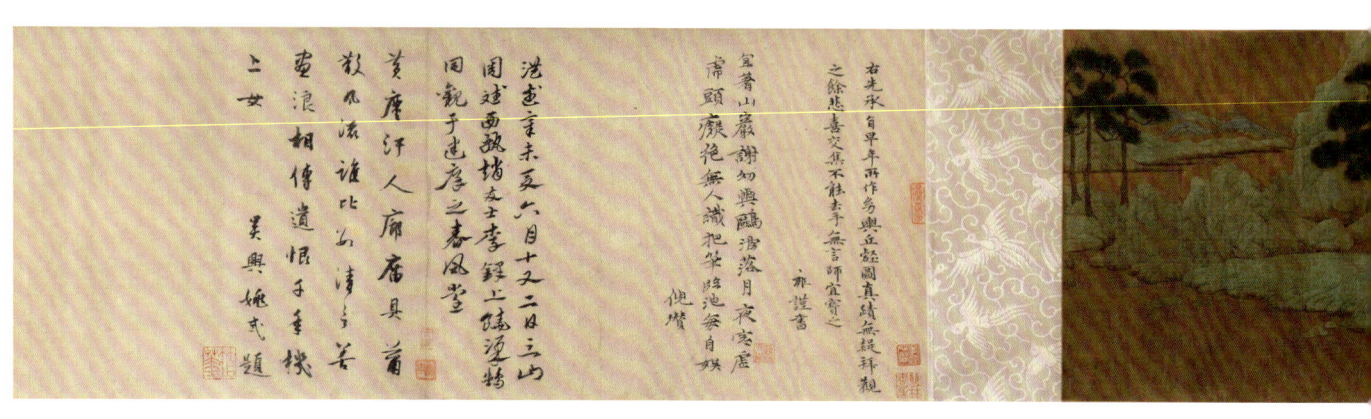

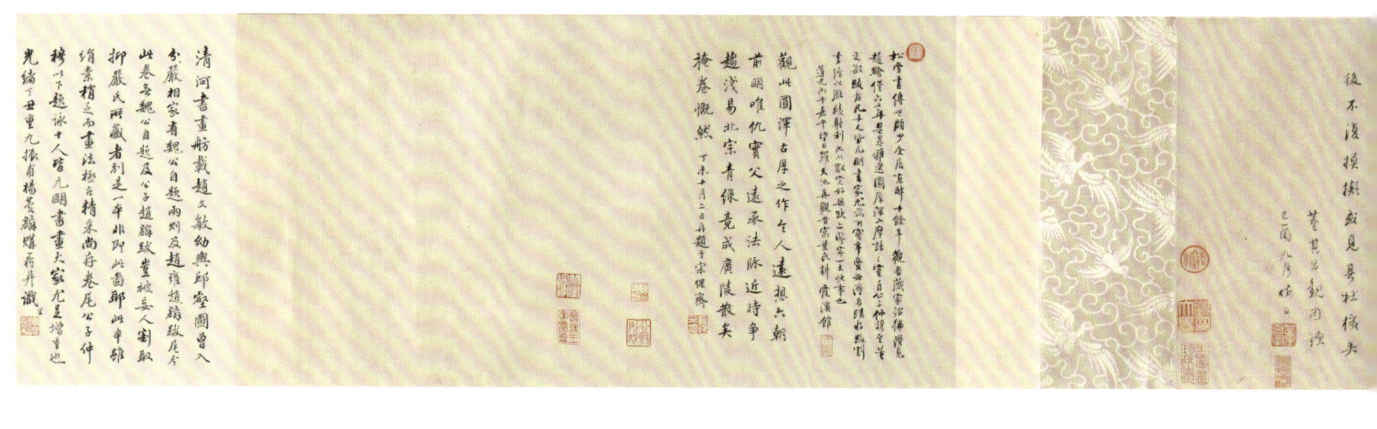

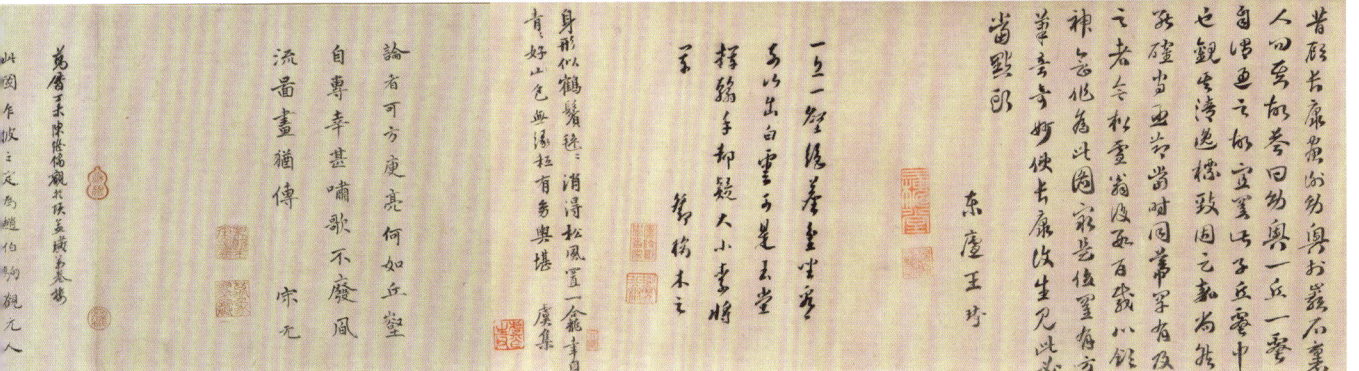

## 11. 谢幼舆丘壑图

元
赵孟頫
绢本设色
手卷
纵27.4、横117厘米
普林斯顿大学美术馆

## Mind Landscape of Xie Youyu

Yuan dynasty (1271–1368)
Zhao Mengfu
Ink and color on silk
Handscroll
H×W : 27.4×117 cm
The Princeton University Art Museum
Edward L. Elliott Family Collection. Museum purchase, Fowler McCormick, Class of 1921, Fund
© 2024. Princeton University Art Museum/Art Resource NY/Scala, Florence

傑自幼小學書之餘時時戲弄小筆於山水獨不能工蓋自唐以來如王右丞大小李將軍鄭虔盧鴻之徒不能一二見至五代荊關董范輩出尤與唐人筆意遊絕儻而作者雖未敢與古人比論視之世畫手則自謂少異耳因野雲求畫故出其末為嫩

### 12. 双松平远图

元
赵孟頫
纸本水墨
手卷
纵26.8、横107.5厘米
大都会艺术博物馆

### Twin Pines, Level Distance

Yuan dynasty (1271–1368)
Zhao Mengfu
Ink on paper
Handscroll
H×W : 26.8×107.5 cm
The Metropolitan Museum of Art
Ex coll.: C. C. Wang Family, Gift of The Dillon Fund, 1973

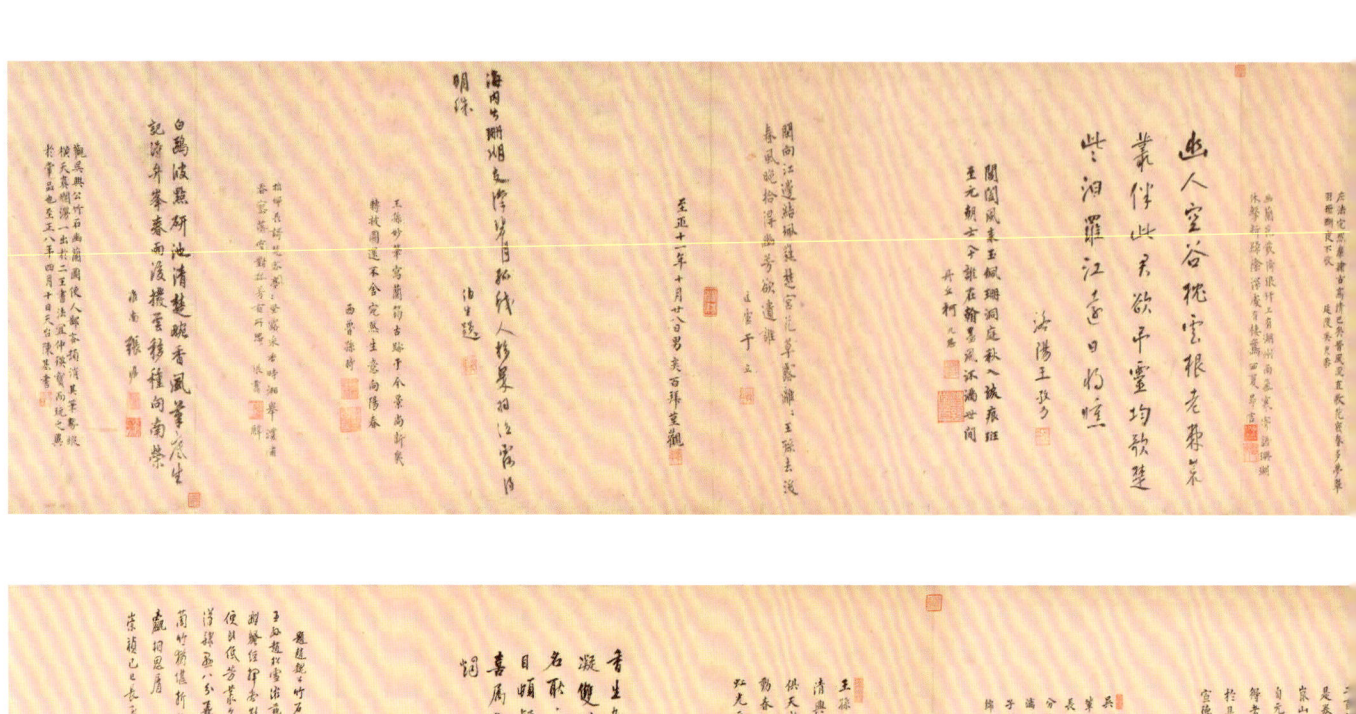

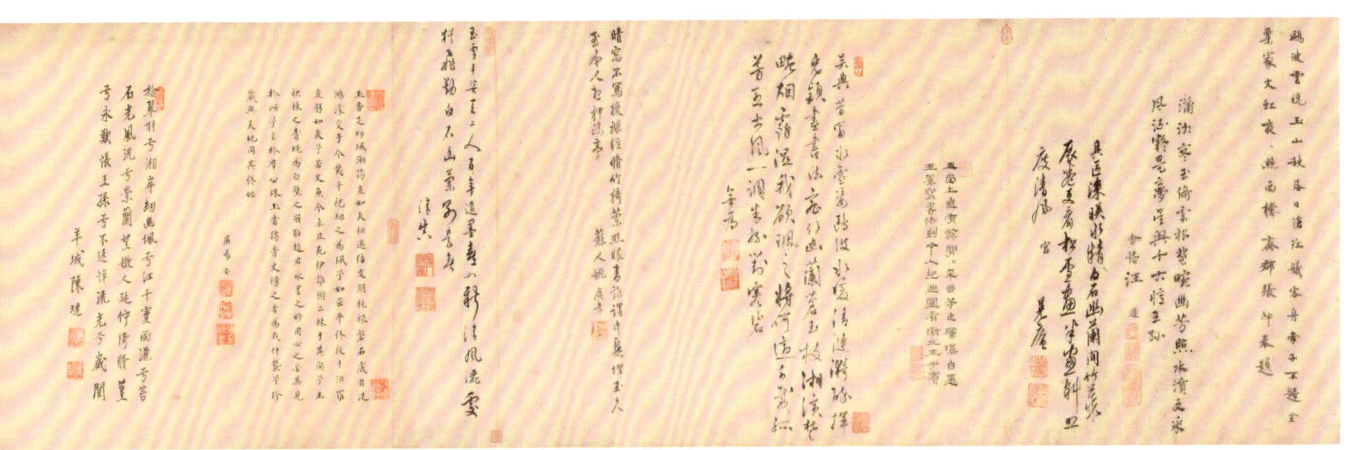

### 13. 竹石幽兰图

元
赵孟頫
纸本水墨
手卷
纵50.9、横147.8厘米
克利夫兰艺术博物馆

### Bamboo, Rocks and Lonely Orchids

Yuan dynasty (1271–1368)
Zhao Mengfu
Ink on paper
Handscroll
H×W : 50.9×147.8 cm
The Cleveland Museum of Art
John L. Severance Fund by exchange

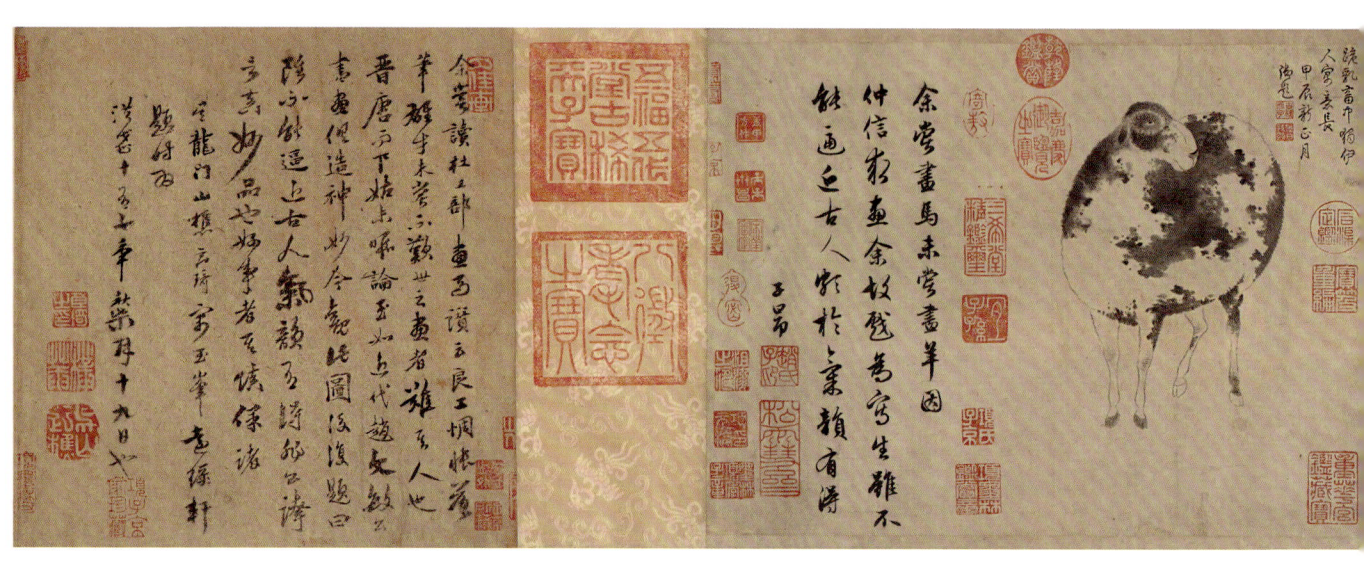

### 14. 二羊图

元
赵孟頫
纸本水墨
手卷
纵25.2、横48.7厘米
弗利尔美术馆

### Sheep and Goat

Yuan dynasty (1271–1368)
Zhao Mengfu
Ink on paper
Handscroll
H×W : 25.2×48.7 cm
The Freer Gallery of Art
Purchase–Charles Lang Freer Endowment

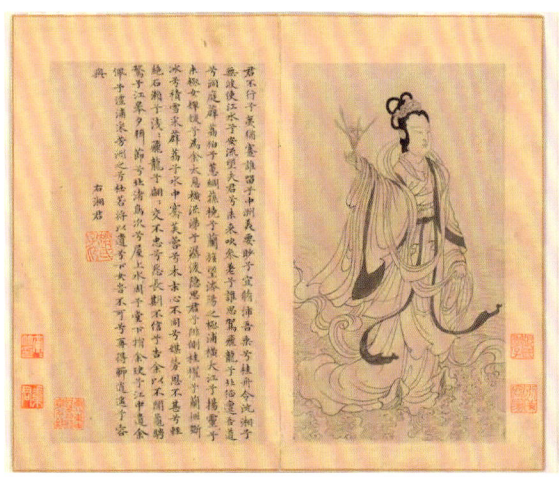
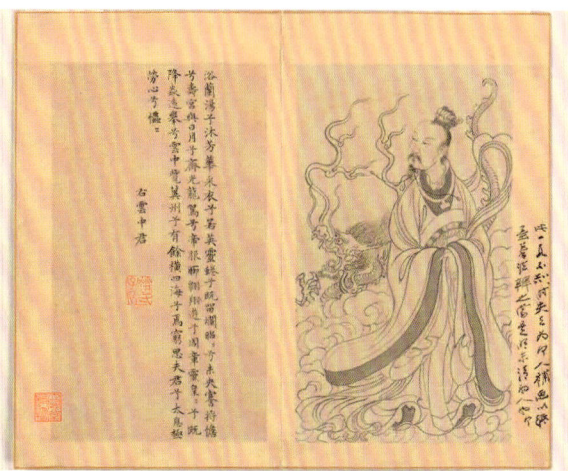
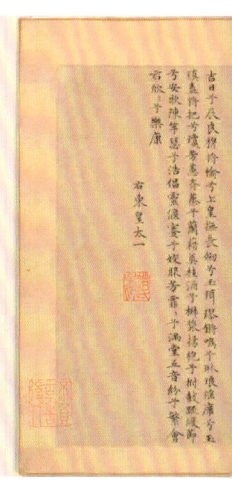

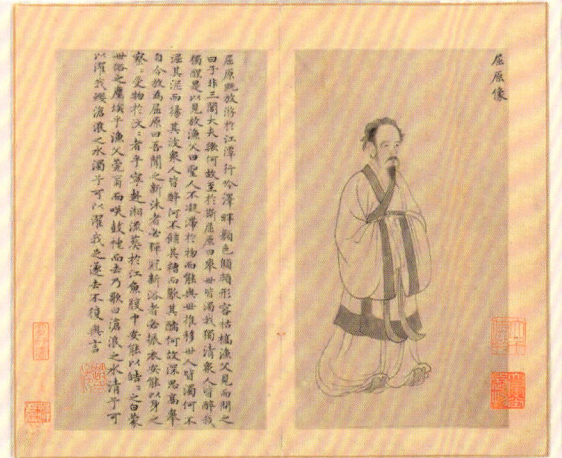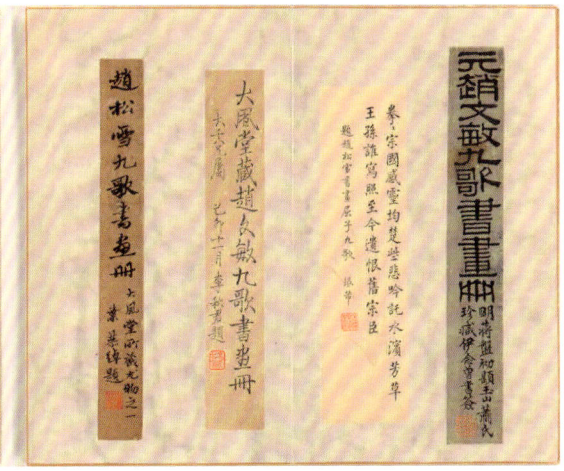

## 15. 九歌图

元
（传）赵孟頫
纸本水墨
册页
每开：纵26.4、横15.9厘米
大都会艺术博物馆

## Nine Songs

Yuan dynasty (1271–1368)
Attributed to Zhao Mengfu
Ink on paper
Album leaf
H×W(each leaf)：26.4×15.9 cm
The Metropolitan Museum of Art
Ex coll.: C. C. Wang Family, Fletcher Fund, 1973

與女遊兮九河衝風起兮橫波乘水車兮荷蓋駕兩龍兮驂螭登崑崙兮四望心飛揚兮浩蕩日將暮兮悵忘歸惟極浦兮寤懷魚鱗屋兮龍堂紫貝闕兮朱宮靈何為兮水中乘白黿兮逐文魚與女遊兮河之渚流澌紛兮將來子交手兮東行送美人兮南浦波滔滔兮來迎魚鄰鄰兮媵予

右河伯

暾將出兮東方照吾檻兮扶桑撫余馬兮安驅夜皎皎兮既明駕龍輈兮乘雷載雲旗兮委蛇長太息兮將上心低佪兮顧懷羌聲色兮娛人觀者憺兮忘歸縆瑟兮交鼓簫鐘兮瑤簴鳴篪兮吹竽思靈保兮賢姱翾飛兮翠曾展詩兮會舞應律兮合節靈之來兮蔽日青雲衣兮白霓裳舉長矢兮射天狼操余弧兮反淪降援北斗兮酌桂漿撰余轡兮高駝翔杳冥冥兮以東行

右東君

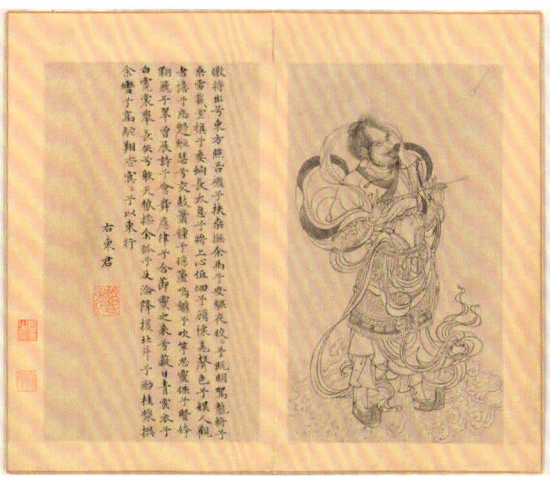

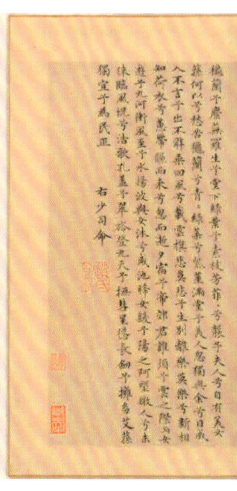

右少司命

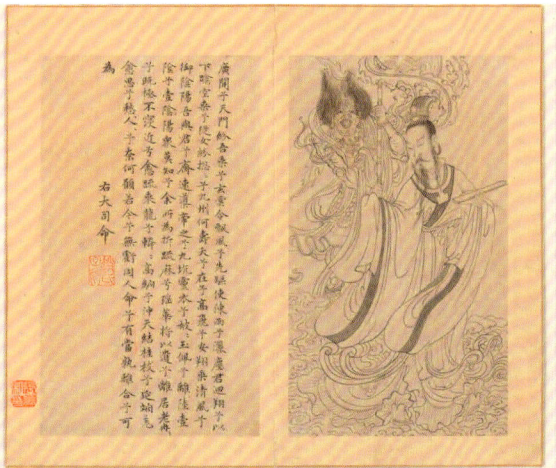

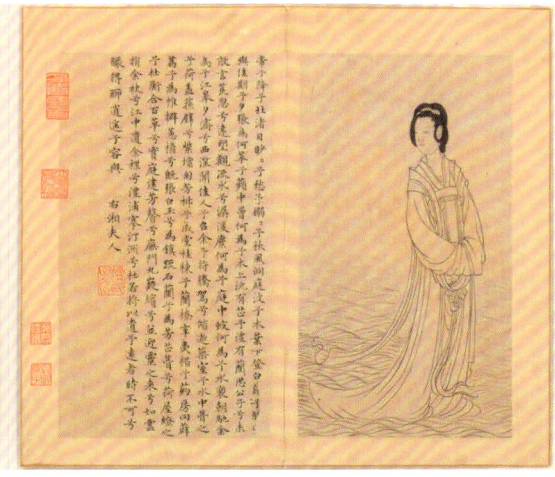

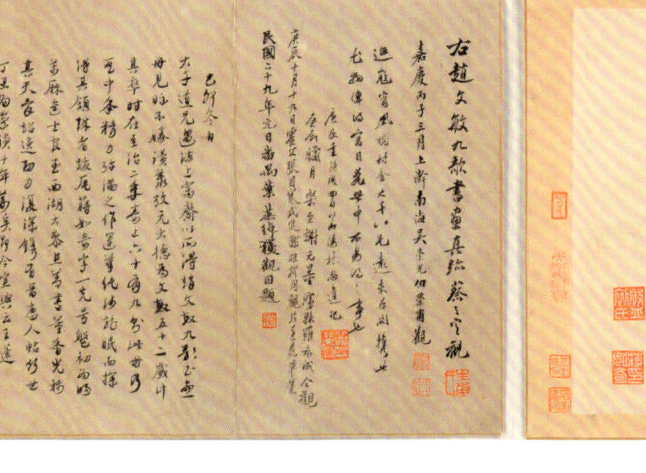

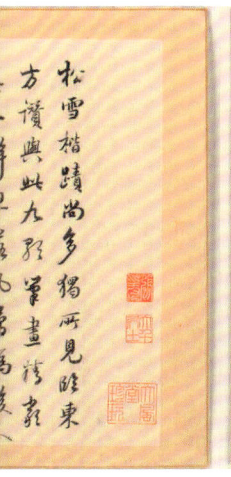 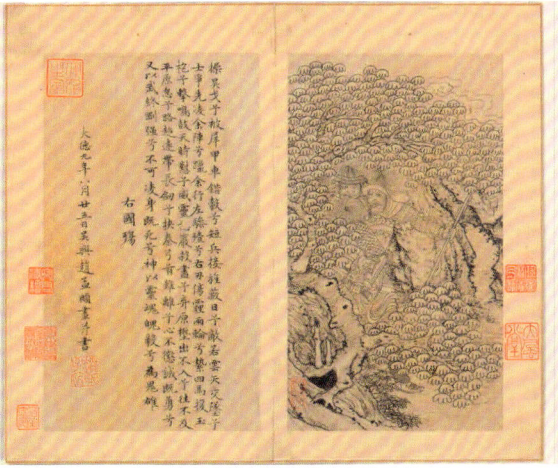 

君不行兮夷猶蹇誰留兮中洲美要眇兮宜修沛吾乘兮桂舟令沅湘兮
無波使江水兮安流望夫君兮未來吹參差兮誰思駕飛龍兮北征邅吾道
兮洞庭薜荔柏兮蕙綢蓀橈兮蘭旌望涔陽之極浦橫大江兮揚靈兮
未極女嬋媛兮為余太息橫流涕兮潺湲隱思君兮陫側桂櫂兮蘭枻斲
冰兮積雪采薜荔兮水中搴芙蓉兮木末心不同兮媒勞恩不甚兮輕
絕石瀨兮淺淺飛龍兮翩翩交不忠兮怨長期不信兮告余以不閒鼂騁
騖兮江皋夕弭節兮北渚鳥次兮屋上水周兮堂下捐余玦兮江中遺余
佩兮澧浦采芳洲之兮杜若將以遺兮下女當不可兮再得聊逍遙兮容
與

右湘君

廣開兮天門紛吾乘兮玄雲令飄風兮先驅使涷雨兮灑塵君迴翔兮以下踰空桑兮從女紛總總兮九州何壽夭兮在予高飛兮安翔乘清風兮御陰陽吾與君兮齋速漢帝之兮九坑靈衣兮披々玉佩兮離陸壹陰兮壹陰陽衆莫知兮余所為折蔬麻兮瑤華將以遺兮離居老冉、兮既極不寖近兮愈跪乘龍兮轔々高駟兮沖天結桂枝兮延蚵羌愈思兮愁人、兮奈何顧若今兮無斁固人命兮有當孰離合兮可為

右大司命

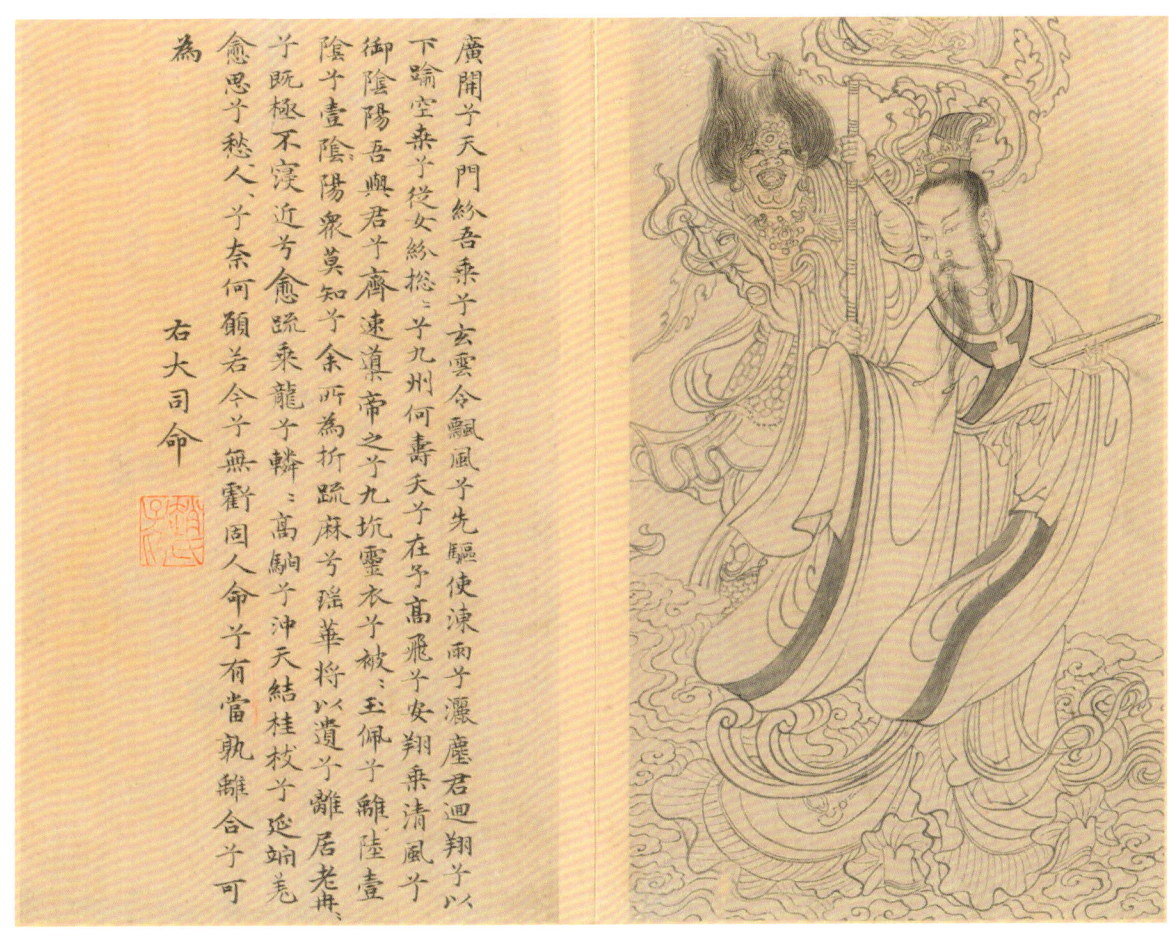

**16. 江村渔乐图**

元
（传）赵孟頫
绢本设色
册页
纵28.6、横30厘米
克利夫兰艺术博物馆

**River Village: Fisherman's Joy**

Yuan dynasty (1271–1368)
Attributed to Zhao Mengfu
Ink and color on silk
Album leaf
H×W : 28.6×30 cm
The Cleveland Museum of Art
Purchase–Charles Lang Freer Endowment

### 17. 墨竹图册

元或明
（传）管道升
绢本水墨
册页
每开：纵22、横22厘米
科隆东亚艺术博物馆

### Bamboo and Poems

Yuan dynasty (1271–1368) or Ming dynasty (1368–1644)
Attributed to Guan Daosheng
Ink on silk
Album leaf
H×W(each leaf)：22×22 cm
The Museum of East Asian Art, Cologne
© Rheinisches Bildarchiv Köln

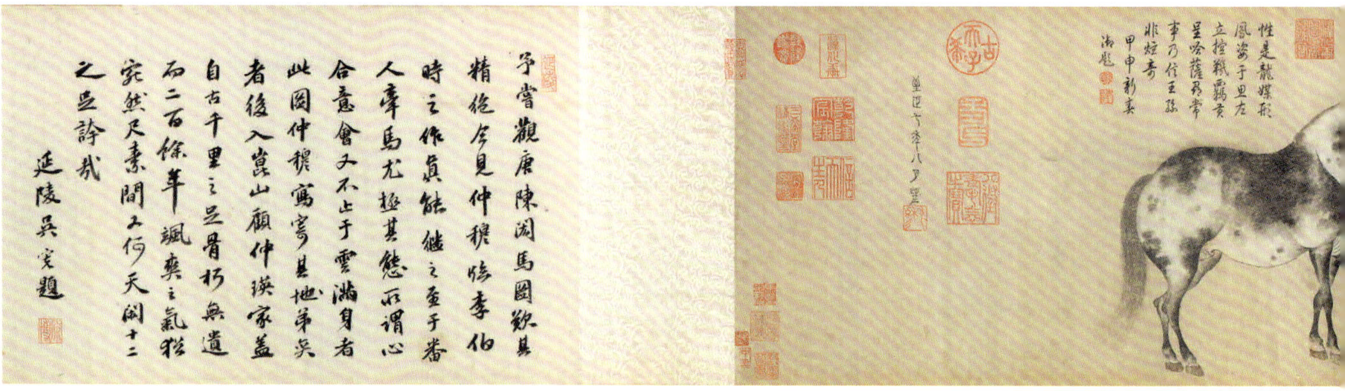

予嘗觀唐陳閎馬圖歎其
精絕今見仲穆臨李伯
時之作真能繼之至于蕃
人牽馬尤極其態所謂心
合意會又不止于雲滿身者
此圖仲穆寫其地弟吳
者後入崑山顧仲瑛家蓋
自古千里之足骨朽無遺
而二百餘年颯爽之氣猶
宛然尺素間又何天閑十二
之足詫我
　延陵吳宽題

**18. 仿李公麟人马图**

元至正七年（1347年）
赵雍
纸本设色
手卷
纵31.5、横73.5厘米
弗利尔美术馆

**Horse and Groom After Li Gonglin**

Yuan dynasty (1271–1368), dated 1347
Zhao Yong
Ink and color on paper
Handscroll
H×W : 31.5×73.5 cm
The Freer Gallery of Art
Purchase–Charles Lang Freer Endowment

050

### 19. 溪山渔隐图

元
（传）赵雍
绢本设色
立轴
纵87.2、横42.8厘米
克利夫兰艺术博物馆

### Fishermen–hermits in Stream and Mountain

Yuan dynasty (1271–1368)
Attributed to Zhao Yong
Ink and color on silk
Hanging scroll
H×W : 87.2×42.8 cm
The Cleveland Museum of Art
Bequest of Mrs. A. Dean Perry 1997.93

#### 20. 番骑图

元至正二十年（1360年）
（传）赵麟
纸本水墨
手卷
纵23.8、横108.3厘米
弗利尔美术馆

### Tartar Horsemen

Yuan dynasty (1271–1368), dated 1360
Attributed to Zhao Lin
Ink on paper
Handscroll
H×W : 23.8×108.3 cm
The Freer Gallery of Art
Purchase–Charles Lang Freer Endowment

054

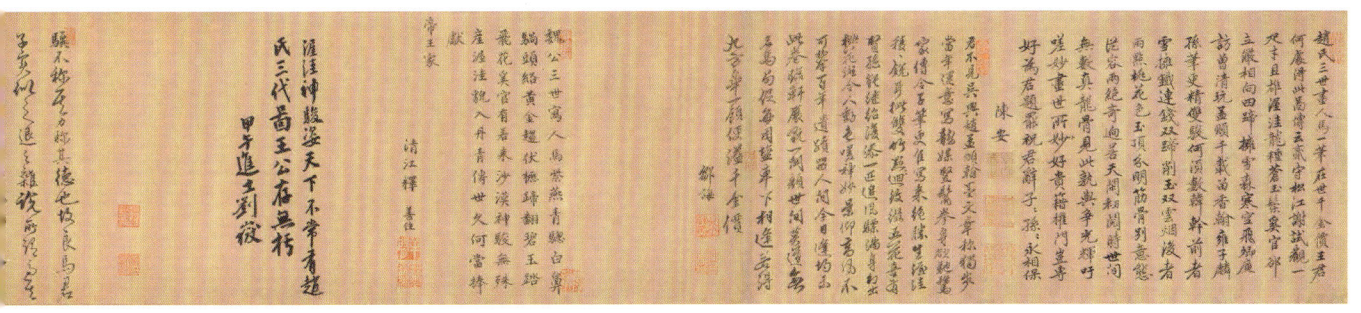

### 21. 赵氏三世人马图

元
赵孟頫、赵雍、赵麟
纸本设色
手卷
纵30.2、横178.1厘米
大都会艺术博物馆

### Grooms and Horses

Yuan dynasty (1271–1368)
Zhao Mengfu, Zhao Yong, Zhao Lin
Ink and color on paper
Handscroll
H×W : 30.2×178.1 cm
The Metropolitan Museum of Art
Gift of John M. Crawford Jr., 1988

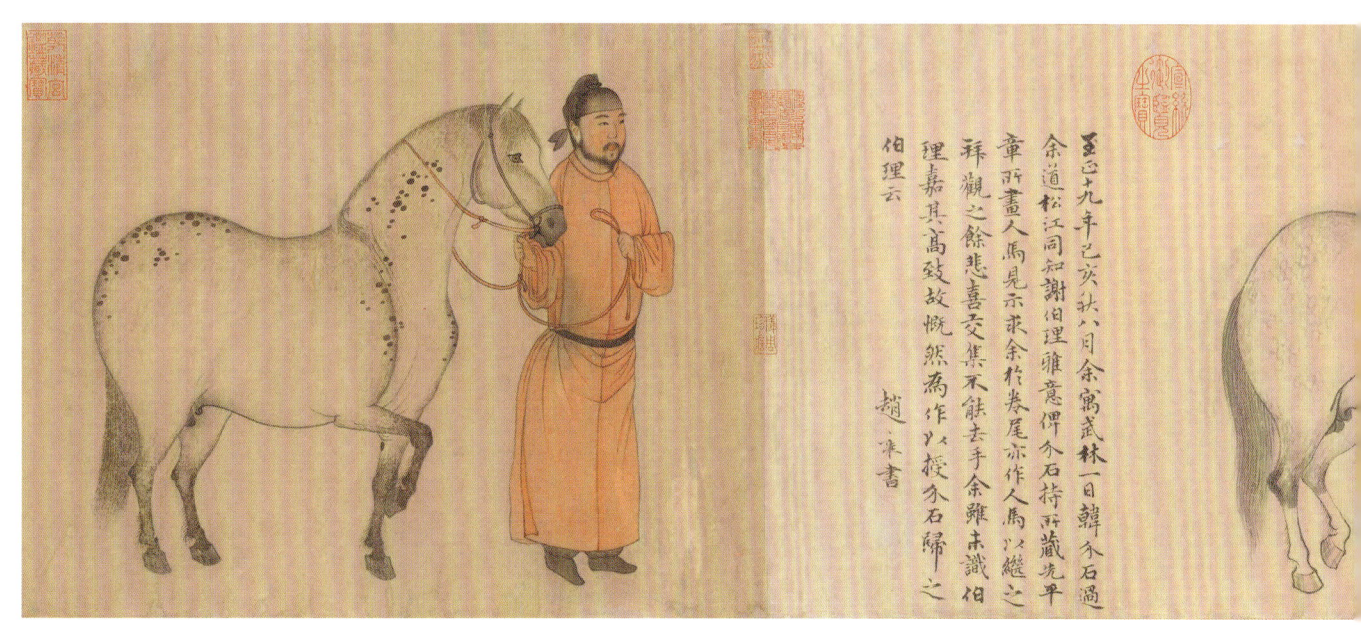

至正九年己亥秋八月余寓武林一日韓介石過
余道松江同知謝伯理雖意佩介石持所藏先平
章所畫人馬見示求余於卷尾亦作人馬以繼之
祥觀之餘悲喜交集余雖去手余雖未識伯
理嘉其高致故慨然為作以授介石歸之
伯理云

趙 麟書

**22. 仿董源夏山图**

元
（传）黄公望
绢本设色
立轴
纵131.7、横55.6厘米
克利夫兰艺术博物馆

**Summer Mountains After Dong Yuan**

Yuan dynasty (1271–1368)
Attributed to Huang Gongwang
Ink and color on silk
Hanging scroll
H×W : 131.7×55.6 cm
The Cleveland Museum of Art
Cornelia Blakemore Warner Bequest, by exchange, and Mr. and Mrs. William H. Marlatt Fund 1992.1

### 23. 老松图

元至元元年（1335年）
吴镇
绢本水墨
立轴
纵166.1、横82.6厘米
大都会艺术博物馆

### Crooked Pine

Yuan dynasty (1271–1368), dated 1335
Wu Zhen
Ink on silk
Hanging scroll
H×W : 166.1×82.6 cm
The Metropolitan Museum of Art
Purchase, The Dillon Fund Gift, 1985

## 24. 渔父图

元
吴镇
纸本水墨
手卷
纵31.1、横53.8厘米
大都会艺术博物馆

## Fisherman

Yuan dynasty (1271–1368)
Wu Zhen
Ink on paper
Handscroll
H×W : 31.1×53.8 cm
The Metropolitan Museum of Art
Bequest of John M. Crawford Jr., 1988

**25. 古木竹石图**

元至元四年（1338年）
（传）吴镇
绢本水墨
立轴
纵166.7、横97.8厘米
大都会艺术博物馆

**Bamboo, Old Tree and Rock**

Yuan dynasty (1271–1368), dated 1338
Attributed to Wu Zhen
Ink on silk
Hanging scroll
H×W : 166.7×97.8 cm
The Metropolitan Museum of Art
Ex coll.: C. C. Wang Family, Gift of Oscar L. Tang Family, 2012

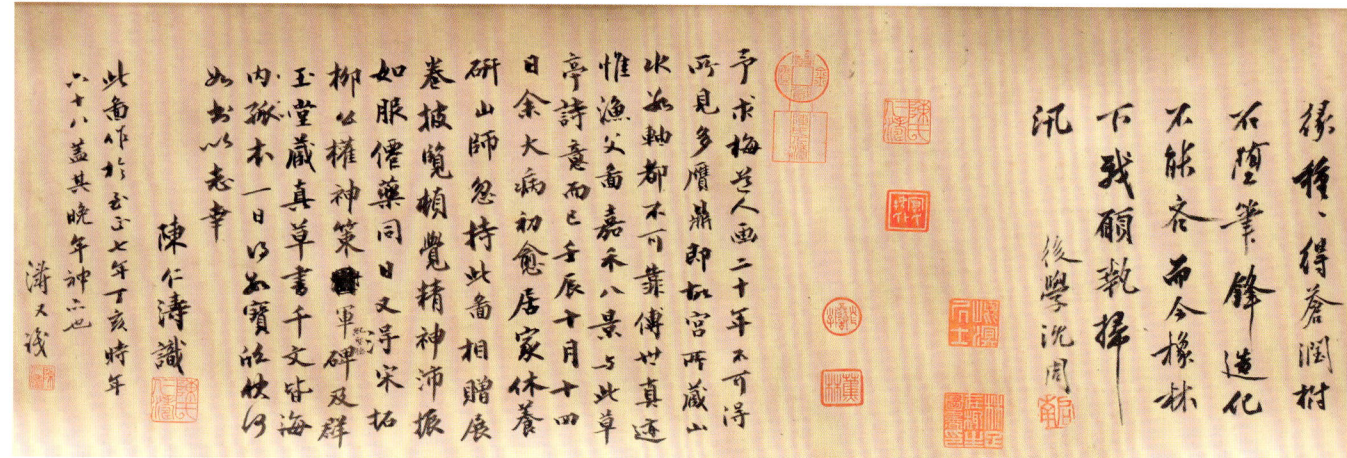

### 26. 草亭诗意图

元至正七年（1347年）
（传）吴镇
纸本水墨
手卷
纵23.8、横99.4厘米
克利夫兰艺术博物馆

### Poetic Feeling in Thatched Pavilion

Yuan dynasty (1271–1368), dated 1347
Attributed to Wu Zhen
Ink on paper
Handscroll
H×W : 23.8×99.4 cm
The Cleveland Museum of Art
Leonard C. Hanna, Jr. Fund 1963.259

**27. 秋林渔隐图**

元至正九年（1349年）
盛懋
绢本设色
册页
纵26.7、横33.7厘米
大都会艺术博物馆

**Recluse Fisherman, Autumn Trees**

Yuan dynasty (1271–1368), dated 1349
Sheng Mao
Ink and color on silk
Album leaf
H×W : 26.7×33.7 cm
The Metropolitan Museum of Art
Ex coll.: C. C. Wang Family, Purchase, Florance Waterbury Bequest and Gift of Mr. and Mrs. Nathan Cummings, by exchange, 1973

### 28. 秋林渔隐图

元至正十年（1350年）
盛懋
纸本水墨
立轴
纵102.6、横33.3厘米
大都会艺术博物馆

### Recluse Fishing by Autumn Trees

Yuan dynasty (1271–1368), dated 1350
Sheng Mao
Ink on paper
Hanging scroll
H×W : 102.6×33.3 cm
The Metropolitan Museum of Art
Bequest of John M. Crawford Jr., 1988

### 29. 秋山行旅图

元
盛懋
绢本设色
册页
纵24.4、横26.5厘米
克利夫兰艺术博物馆

### Travelers in Autumn Mountains

Yuan dynasty (1271–1368)
Sheng Mao
Ink and color on silk
Album leaf
H×W : 24.4×26.5 cm
The Cleveland Museum of Art
Gift of Mr. and Mrs. Severance A. Millikin
1963.589

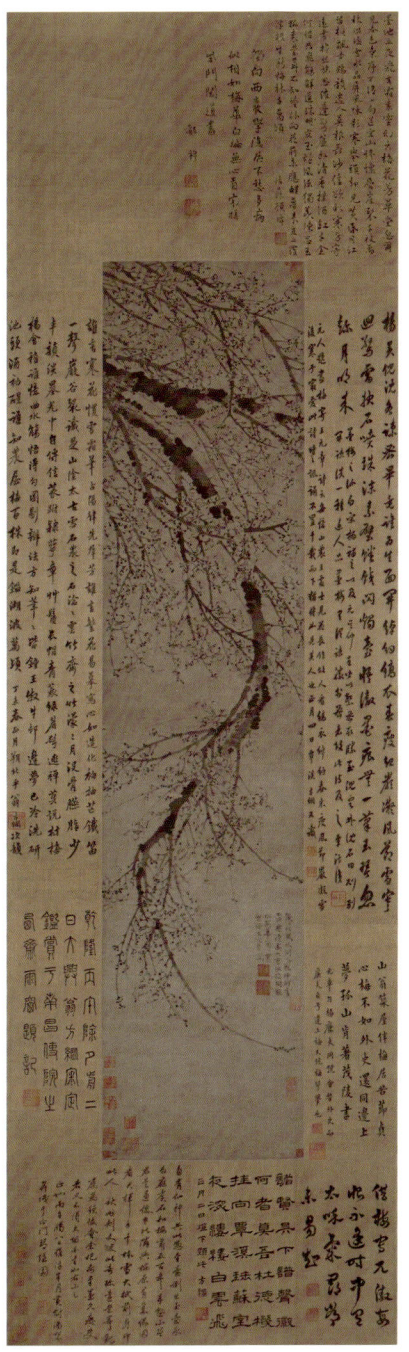

### 30. 墨梅图

元
王冕
纸本水墨
立轴
纵114.8、横26厘米
耶鲁大学艺术博物馆

### Ink Plum

Yuan dynasty (1271–1368)
Wang Mian
Ink on paper
Hanging scroll
H×W : 114.8×26 cm
The Yale University Art Gallery
Hobart and Edward Small Moore Memorial
Collection, Gift of Mrs. William H. Moore

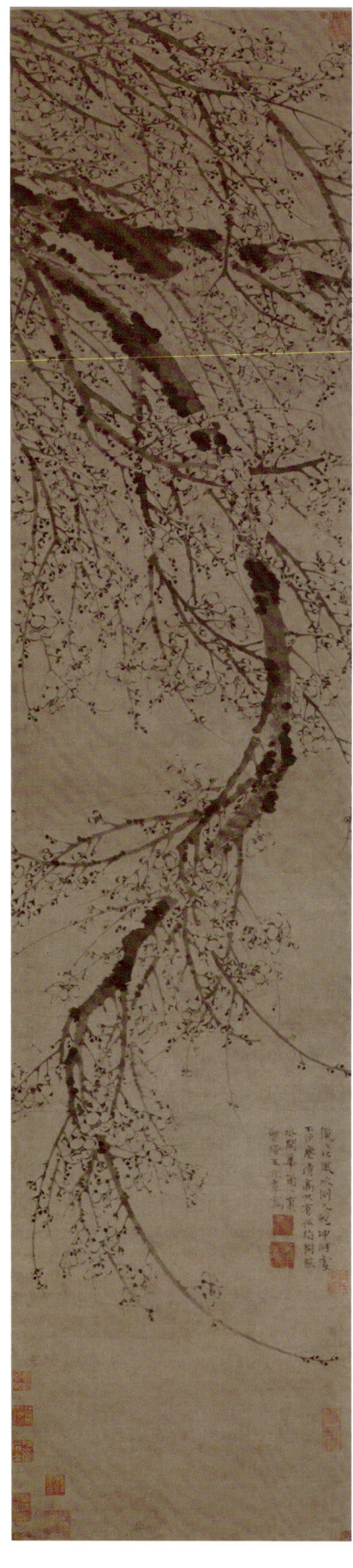

**31. 墨梅图**

元
王冕
绢本水墨
立轴
纵113、横50.2厘米
大都会艺术博物馆

**Fragrant Snow at Broken Bridge**

Yuan dynasty (1271–1368)
Wang Mian
Ink on silk
Hanging scroll
H×W : 113×50.2 cm
The Metropolitan Museum of Art
Ex coll.: C. C. Wang Family, Purchase, Gift of J. Pierpont Morgan, by exchange, 1973

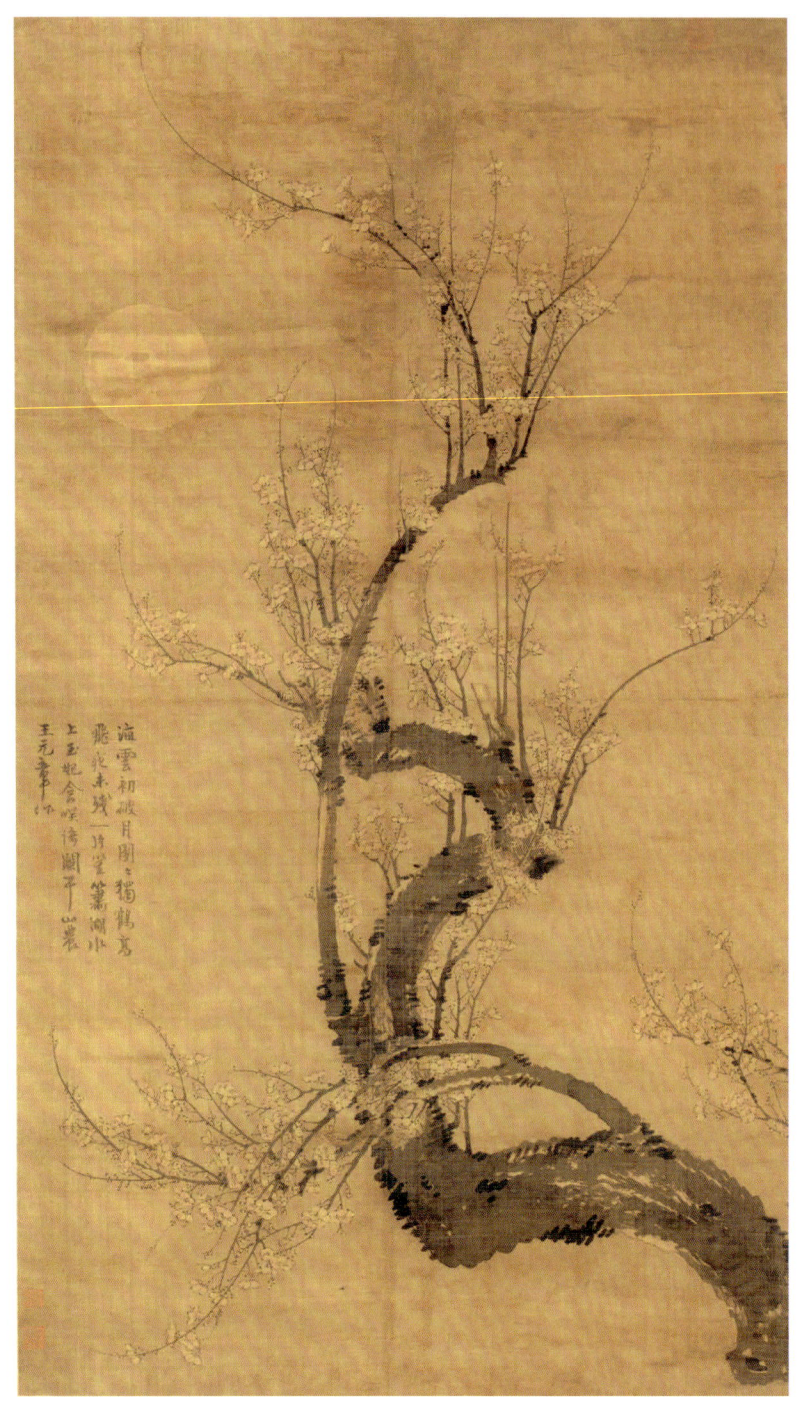

**32. 梅月图**

元
王冕
绢本水墨
立轴
纵164.6、横94.6厘米
克利夫兰艺术博物馆

**Prunus in Moonlight**

Yuan dynasty (1271–1368)
Wang Mian
Ink on silk
Hanging scroll
H×W : 164.6×94.6 cm
The Cleveland Museum of Art
Leonard C. Hanna, Jr. Fund 1974.26

### 33. 树石图

元
曹知白
绢本设色
立轴
纵27.4、横27.3厘米
普林斯顿大学美术馆

### Rocks and Trees

Yuan dynasty (1271–1368)
Cao Zhibai
Ink and color on silk
Hanging scroll
H×W : 27.4×27.3 cm
The Princeton University Art Museum
Museum purchase, John Maclean Magie, Class of 1892, and Gertrude Magie Fund
© 2024. Princeton University Art Museum/Art Resource NY/Scala, Florence

## 34. 王维诗意图

元至治三年（1323年）
唐棣
绢本设色
立轴
纵128.9、横68.7厘米
大都会艺术博物馆

### Landscape After Poem by Wang Wei

Yuan dynasty (1271–1368), dated 1323
Tang Di
Ink and color on silk
Hanging scroll
H×W : 128.9×68.7 cm
The Metropolitan Museum of Art
Gift of Ernest Erickson Foundation, 1985

**35. 霜浦归渔图**

元至正二年（1342年）
唐棣
绢本设色
立轴
纵134.3、横86厘米
大都会艺术博物馆

**Returning Fishermen**

Yuan dynasty (1271–1368), dated 1342
Tang Di
Ink and color on silk
Hanging scroll
H×W : 134.3×86 cm
The Metropolitan Museum of Art
Ex coll.: C. C. Wang Family, Purchase, Bequest of
Joseph H. Durkee, by exchange, 1973

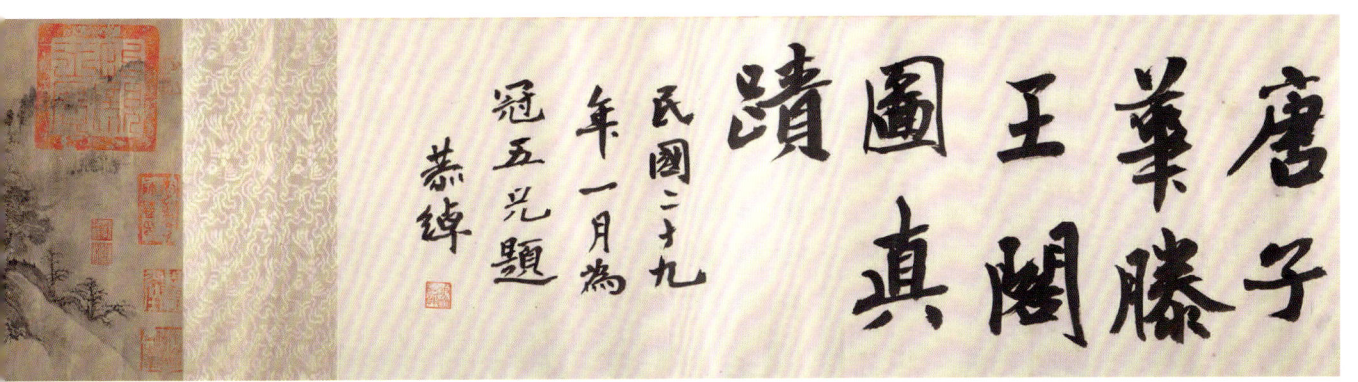

### 36. 滕王阁图

元至正十二年（1352年）
（传）唐棣
纸本水墨
手卷
纵27.5、横84.5厘米
大都会艺术博物馆

### Pavilion of Prince Teng

Yuan dynasty (1271–1368), dated 1352
Attributed to Tang Di
Ink on paper
Handscroll
H×W : 27.5 ×84.5 cm
The Metropolitan Museum of Art
Bequest of John M. Crawford Jr., 1988

**37. 古木寒鸦图**

元
罗稚川
绢本设色
立轴
纵132.1、横80.3厘米
大都会艺术博物馆

**Crows in Old Trees**

Yuan dynasty (1271–1368)
Luo Zhichuan
Ink and color on silk
Hanging scroll
H×W : 132.1×80.3 cm
The Metropolitan Museum of Art
Ex coll.: C. C. Wang Family, Purchase, Gift of J. Pierpont Morgan, by exchange, 1973

**38. 溪桥策杖图**

元
罗稚川
绢本水墨
册页
纵24.5、横25.2厘米
克利夫兰艺术博物馆

**Ramblers over Winding Stream**

Yuan dynasty (1271–1368)
Luo Zhichuan
Ink on silk
Album leaf
H×W : 24.5×25.2 cm
The Cleveland Museum of Art
Gift of the John Huntington Art and Polytechnic
Trust 1915.536

**39. 携琴访友图**      **Carrying Qin on Visit**

元  
（传）罗稚川  
绢本水墨  
立轴  
纵80.8、横35.3厘米  
克利夫兰艺术博物馆

Yuan dynasty (1271–1368)  
Attributed to Luo Zhichuan  
Ink on silk  
Hanging scroll  
H×W : 80.8×35.3 cm  
The Cleveland Museum of Art  
General Income Fund 1919.974

#### 40. 雪山行旅图

元
姚廷美
绢本水墨
立轴
纵98.4、横54.6厘米
大都会艺术博物馆

#### Traveling through Snow-covered Mountains

Yuan dynasty (1271–1368)
Yao Tingmei
Ink on silk
Hanging scroll
H×W : 98.4×54.6 cm
The Metropolitan Museum of Art
Ex coll.: C. C. Wang Family, Gift of Oscar L. Tang Family, 2011

至正廿年春正月日作此倚柔鄉語于庭
世倫人遠悶㯋闌滿院松陰白晝閒
眼底浮塵歸忌却束看流水卧看
山吳興姚逵賛

地僻柴門徧落花鉤簾
鷗雪滿㽪沙鳥絲小楷見
童慣白髮耽吟歲月賒迷
蝶竊香將午夢仰蜂黏
絮散晨徛卽遊阮畫經
行遠醉入天台劉阮家
小海生張俊德

授閒江上避芳蹊茆屋三間白板扉
闢徑柳陰將鶴舞鑿池花外育魚
飛英雄蟻鬪時夢富貴蠟螢事
非睡起草堂新酒熟醉吟明月上
人衣
西夏郭吉

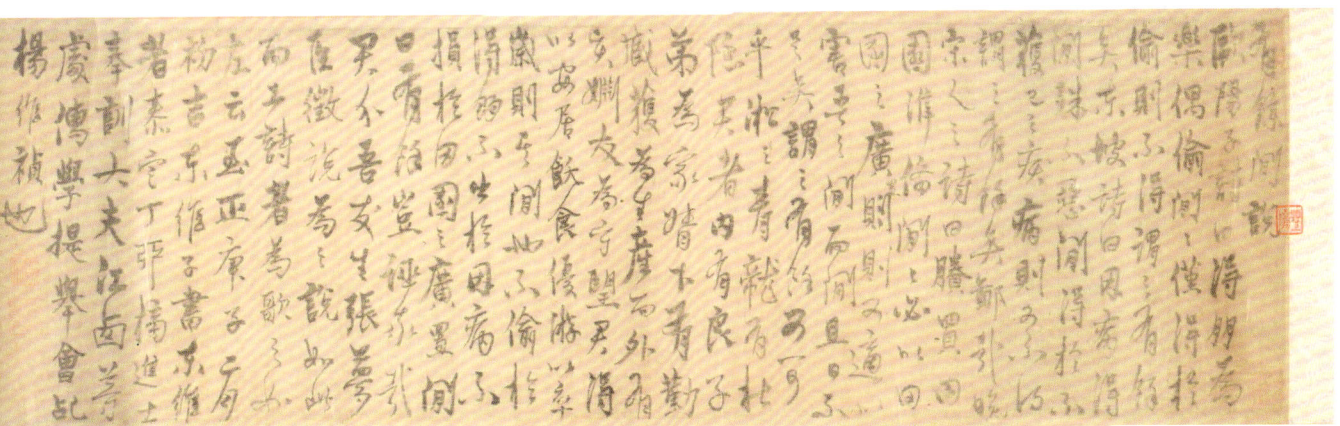

**41. 有余闲图**

元至正二十年（1360年）
姚廷美
纸本水墨
手卷
纵23.8、横84厘米
克利夫兰艺术博物馆

**Leisure Enough to Spare**

Yuan dynasty (1271–1368), dated 1360
Yao Tingmei
Ink on paper
Handscroll
H×W : 23.8×84 cm
The Cleveland Museum of Art
John L. Severance Fund 1954.791

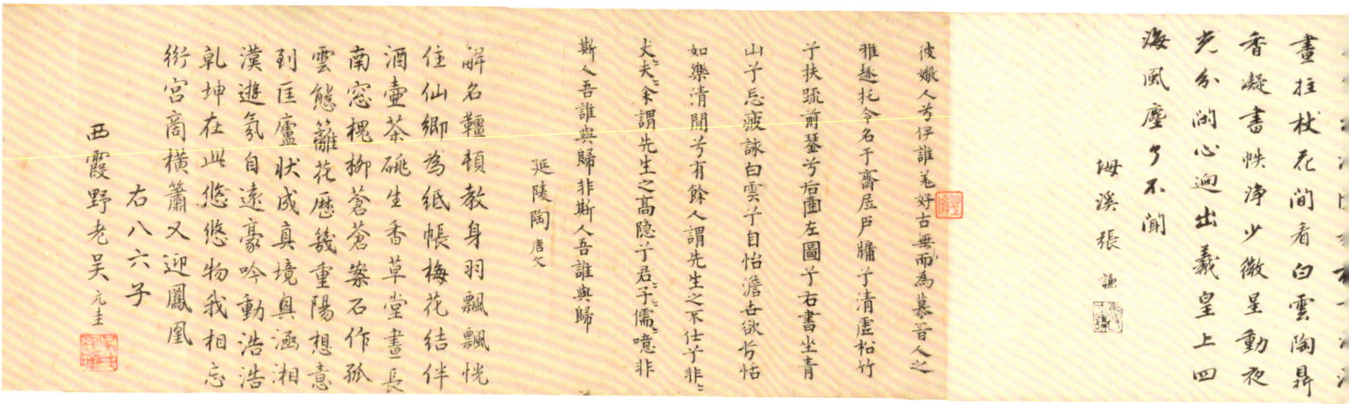

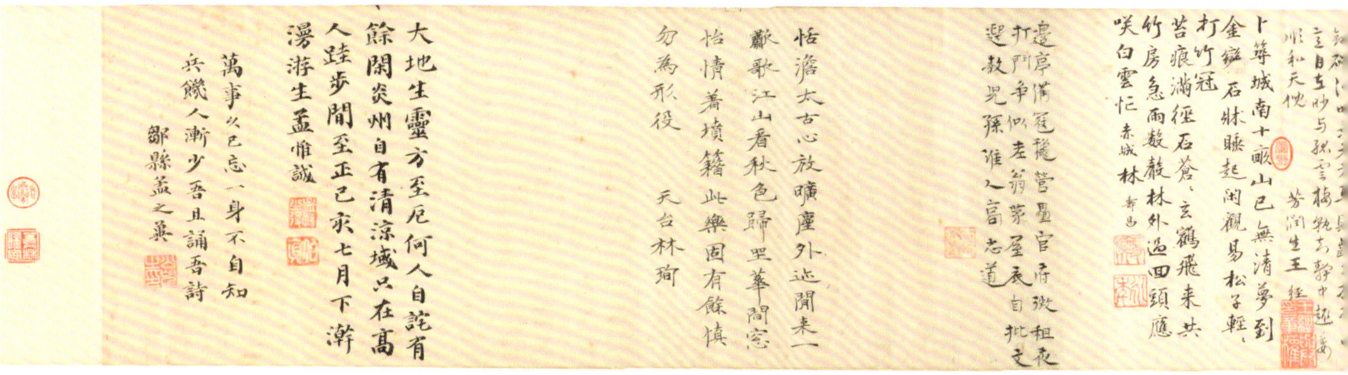

畫挂杖花間看白雲陶鼎
香凝書帙淨少微星動夜
光分澗心迥出羲皇上四
海風塵了不聞
　　　　　　梅溪張逸

使嫩人芳伊誰若對古無而為暴音人之
雅趣託令名于齋居戶牖了清虛柏竹
于扶疎前鑒芳后圖左圖了右書坐青
山了忘渡詠白雲了自怡澹古欲兮恬
如樂清閒芳有餘人謂先生之不仕兮非
犬夫余謂先生之高隱了君子儒噫非
斯人吾誰與歸非斯人吾誰與歸
　　　　　　延陵陶唐文

解名韁頓教身羽飄飄恍
住仙鄉為紙帳梅花結伴
酒壺茶碾生香草堂晝長
南窗槐柳蒼蒼察石作孤
雲態籬花歷錢重陽想意
到匡廬狀成真境具涵湘
漢遊氣自遠豪吟動浩浩
乾坤在此悠悠物我相忘
術宮高橫簫又迎鳳凰
　　右八六子
　　　　　　丑霞野老吳元圭

上等城南十畒山巴無清夢到
金鍾石牀聽起閒觀易松子輕
打竹冠苔痕滿徑石蒼玄鶴飛來共
苦竹房急嗽龕林外迴田頭應
笑白雲忙　　　赤城林壽昌

知亭□冠籠管星官府班租夜
打門爭如老翁茅星辰自批之
迎敕兒孫誰人富志道

恬澹太古心放曠塵外逍閒來一
獻歌江山看秋色歸里華問窓
怡情善境籍此樂固有餘慎
勿為形役
　　　　　　天台林珂

大地生靈方至厄何人自詫有
餘閒炎州自有清涼域六在高
人跬步間至正已亥七月下澣
湯游生盂惟誠

萬事久已忘一身不自知
兵燹人漸少吾且誦吾詩
　　　　　　鄞縣盃之裏

富貴非吾願頤進徒此身兵
戈昏蓮旅天地一遺民茅屋
碧山下釣然秋水濱區。種
桃者莫話武陵春
　　崇德徐士全

一十杜陵雙鬢經自言無浸事
驅馳常依竹徑聽鳴鶴更對雲
山吟好詩滿目黃塵連戰伐當
天赤日苦轅軻不如棄散高清
庄彷彿風前詠采芝
　　吳郡高玉

世路黃塵十丈深切名半帶傍螢心鐵甲裳
軍旁行為何如高隱吾山水明月清風四時
支夫莪芽佳卯如半彼容心事家軍書
蒲散生涯一臺酒底格浮夷實足之優
淮自可怡朝暉看雲無事紫門不魯杜笑鉤兒稱
松下看白雲無事紫門拾瑤草管時
蘇永舜從渠官廟急往征自向閒中說
今古
　　天台李明辰

僻境輪蹄寡安居水竹
幽軒窗時寄傲杖屨或
邀遊松下聽玄鶴江邊
友白鷗此生無一事醉
後更歡謳
　　雲東呂辭

彼市彼朝我林我丘彼競
彼趨我且優游嚶舐今榮
何足求竹林茗碗音雲
曾居丘壑志不受軒冕居
低是槳隱客宦寰將焉如
浮鹽陽苞煙
　　下學工造

卜築溪屋畫長閒有餘閒尊
留客醉閉戶課兒書尘
臥香雲捲卻更無軒冕甘
分學樵漁
　　信都馬蹇義

朝陳經濟術夕運改代籌何如
隱君子袖手百不憂居間樂天
性樹德貽孫謀興末己清唯醉
束茶滿甌塵家自擾他何時又
巢由引瓢挂高樹犢避下流
克舜且不事況復為他求
田園遺子孫心遠已脫俗
須論但特詩酒娛賓客莫買
人世蕭閒真足黃浮雲富貴不
應日高猶自擁紫門嗟余
奔走紅塵久亦欲幽樓且
避喧
　　括蒼林茲

語溪顧庠擧

至正廿年春正月日作此併系鄙語于尾

也偏人遠問柴關滿院松陰白晝閒
眼底紅塵歸去卻半看流水臥看
山吳興姚廷美畫

## 42. 墨竹图

元
顾安
纸本水墨
立轴
纵113.7、横33.2厘米
辛辛那提艺术博物馆

## Bamboo

Yuan dynasty (1271–1368)
Gu An
Ink on paper
Hanging scroll
H×W : 113.7×33.2 cm
The Cincinnati Art Museum
John J. Emery Endowment and Fanny Bryce Lehmer Fund
© Bridgeman Images

**43. 仿文同墨竹图**

元至正三年（1343年）
柯九思
绢本水墨
立轴
纵107.6、横47.6厘米
大都会艺术博物馆

**Bamboo After Wen Tong**

Yuan dynasty (1271–1368), dated 1343
Ke Jiusi
Ink on silk
Hanging scroll
H×W : 107.6×47.6 cm
The Metropolitan Museum of Art
 Ex coll.: C. C. Wang Family, Gift of Oscar L. Tang Family, 2006

## 44. 秋林野兴图

元至元五年（1339年）
倪瓒
纸本水墨
立轴
纵98.1、横68.9厘米
大都会艺术博物馆

**Enjoying Wilderness in Autumn Grove**

Yuan dynasty (1271–1368), dated 1339
Ni Zan
Ink on paper
Hanging scroll
H×W : 98.1×68.9 cm
The Metropolitan Museum of Art
Bequest of John M. Crawford Jr., 1988

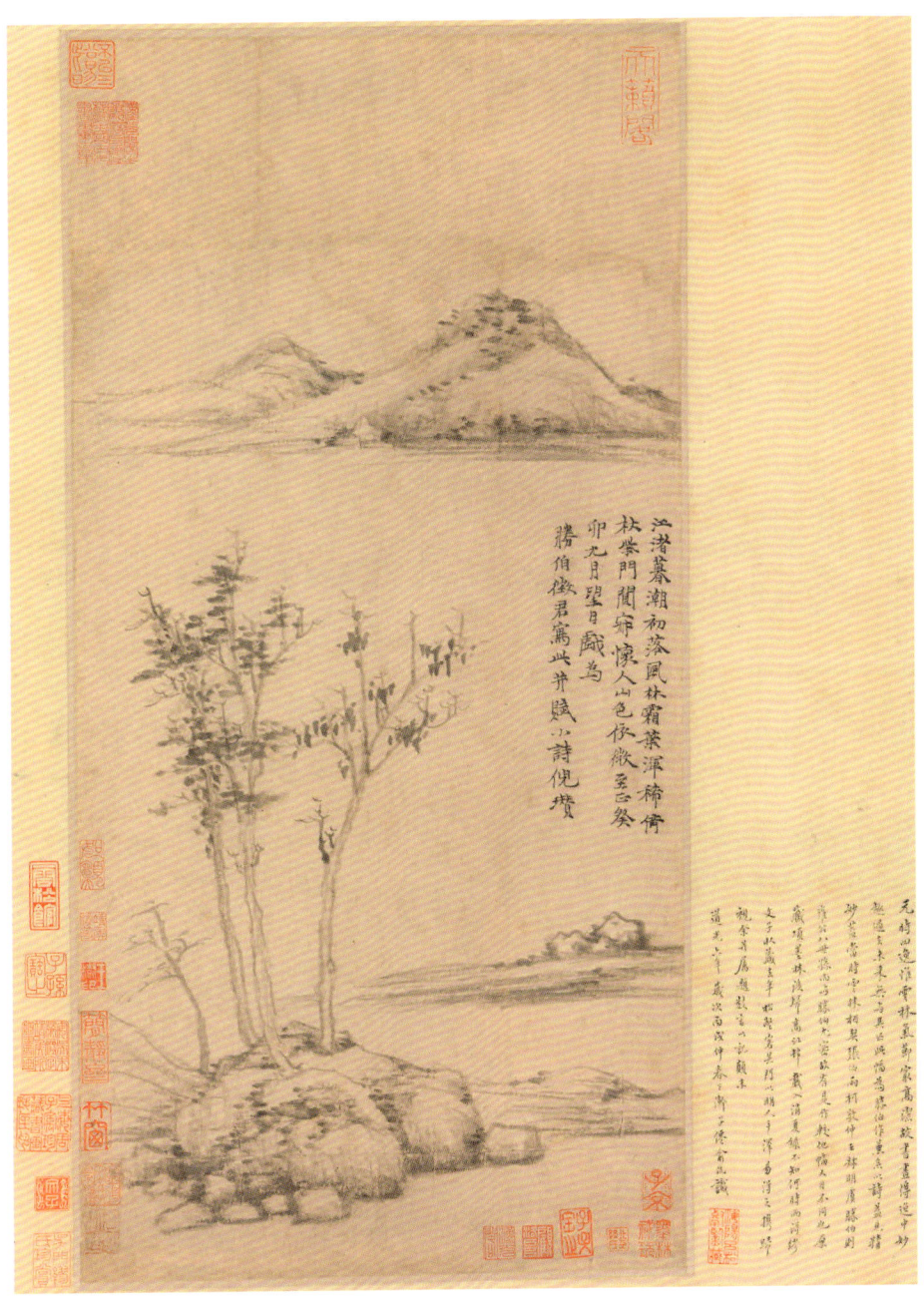

### 45. 江渚风林图

元至正十三年（1353年）
倪瓒
纸本水墨
立轴
纵59.1、横31.1厘米
大都会艺术博物馆

### Wind Among Trees on Riverbank

Yuan dynasty (1271–1368), dated 1353
Ni Zan
Ink on paper
Hanging scroll
H×W : 59.1×31.1 cm
The Metropolitan Museum of Art
Bequest of John M. Crawford Jr., 1988

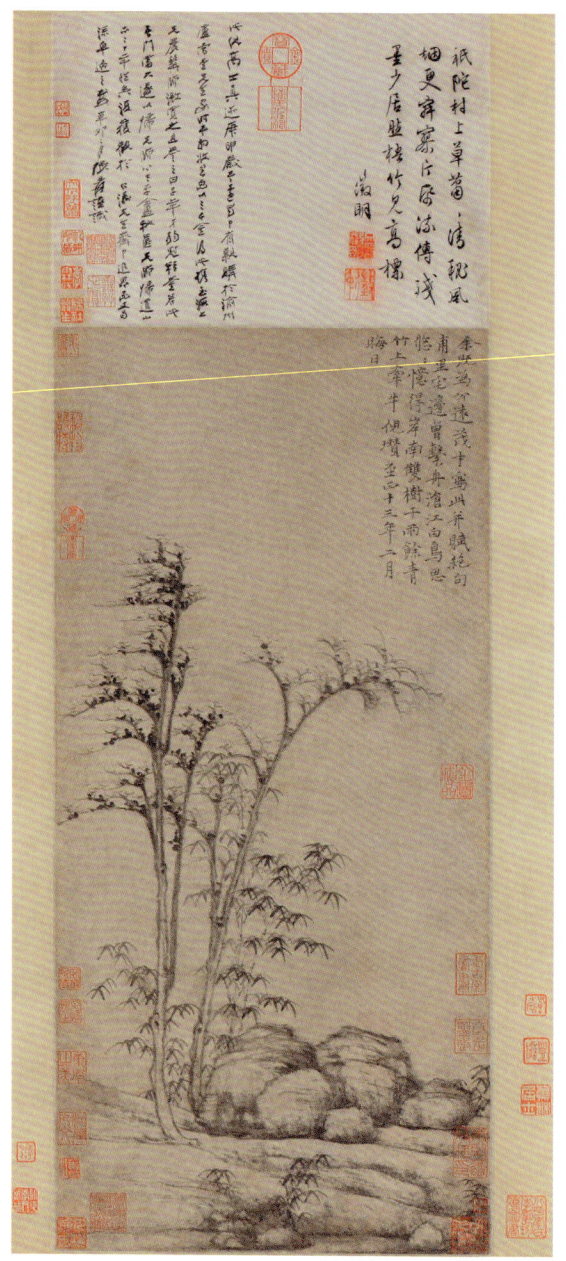

### 46. 岸南双树图

元至正十三年（1353年）
倪瓒
纸本水墨
立轴
纵56、横27厘米
普林斯顿大学美术馆

### Twin Trees by South Bank

Yuan dynasty (1271–1368), dated 1353
Ni Zan
Ink on paper
Hanging scroll
H×W : 56×27 cm
The Princeton University Art Museum
Gift of Wen C. Fong, Class of 1951 and Graduate School Class of 1958, and Constance Tang Fong in honor of Mrs. Edward L. Elliott
© 2024. Princeton University Art Museum/Art Resource NY/Scala, Florence

### 47. 虞山林壑图

明洪武五年（1372年）
倪瓒
纸本水墨
立轴
纵94.6、横35.9厘米
大都会艺术博物馆

### Woods and Valleys of Mount Yu

Ming dynasty (1368–1644), dated 1372
Ni Zan
Ink on paper
Hanging scroll
H×W : 94.6×35.9 cm
The Metropolitan Museum of Art
Ex coll.: C. C. Wang Family, Gift of The Dillon Fund, 1973

**48. 林堂诗思图**

元明之际
倪瓒
纸本水墨
立轴
纵124、横50.5厘米
芝加哥艺术博物馆

**Poetic Thoughts in Forest Pavilion**

Late Yuan to early Ming dynasty
Ni Zan
Ink on paper
Hanging scroll
H×W : 124×50.5 cm
The Art Institute of Chicago
Kate S. Buckingham Endowment; purchased with funds provided by of the E. Rhodes and Leona B. Carpenter Foundation
© 2024. The Art Institute of Chicago / Art Resource, NY/ Scala, Florence

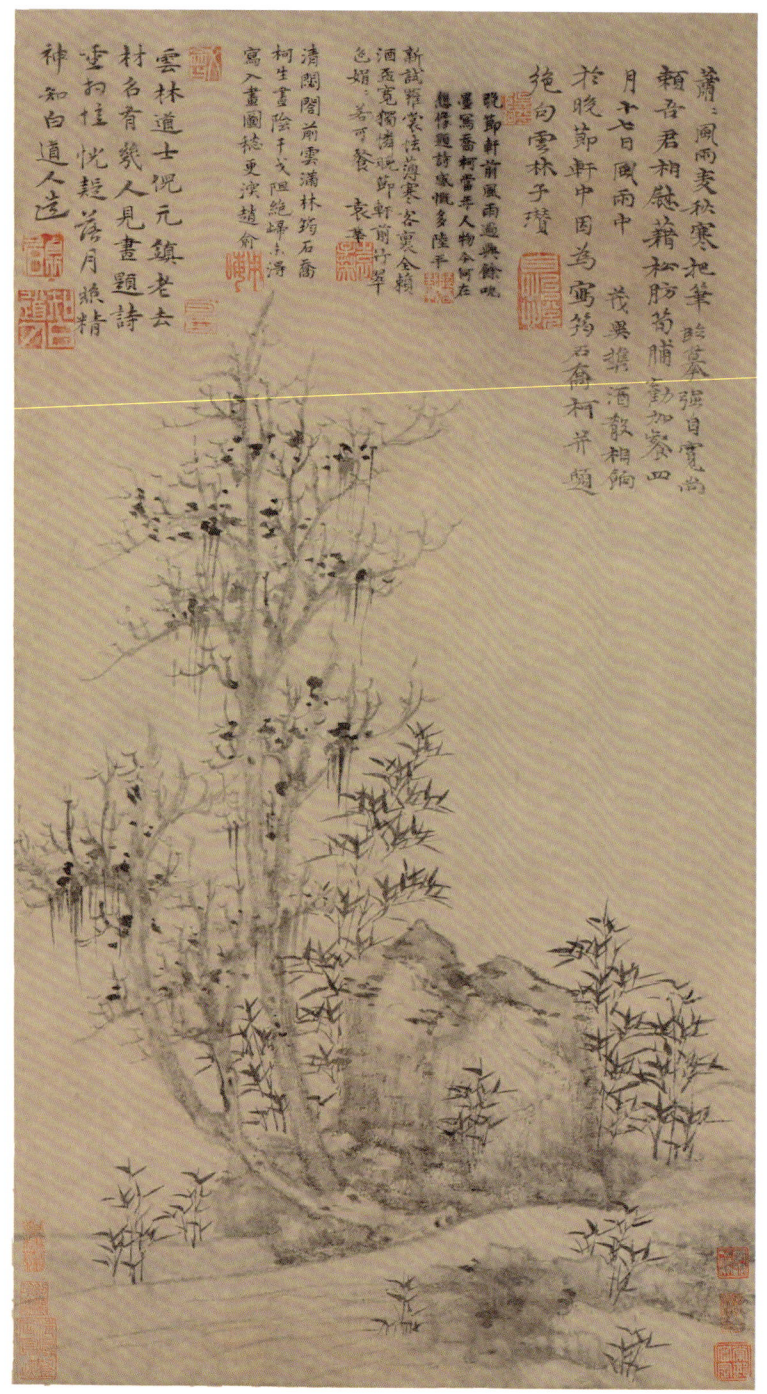

### 49. 筠石乔柯图

元
倪瓒
纸本水墨
立轴
纵67.3、横36.8厘米
克利夫兰艺术博物馆

### Bamboo, Rock and Tall Tree

Yuan dynasty (1271–1368)
Ni Zan
Ink on paper
Hanging scroll
H×W : 67.3×36.8 cm
The Cleveland Museum of Art
Leonard C. Hanna, Jr. Fund 1978.65

#### 50. 墨竹图

元
倪瓒
纸本水墨
册页
纵29.3、横29厘米
弗利尔美术馆

#### Branch of Bamboo

Yuan dynasty (1271–1368)
Ni Zan
Ink on paper
Album leaf
H×W : 29.3×29 cm
The Freer Gallery of Art
Gift of Charles Lang Freer

翰林院侍詔
國史官長沙李東陽書
於玉綸餘中

壬子歲三月廿四日東海倪瓚為
彥明作時寄孝常王達善回篆

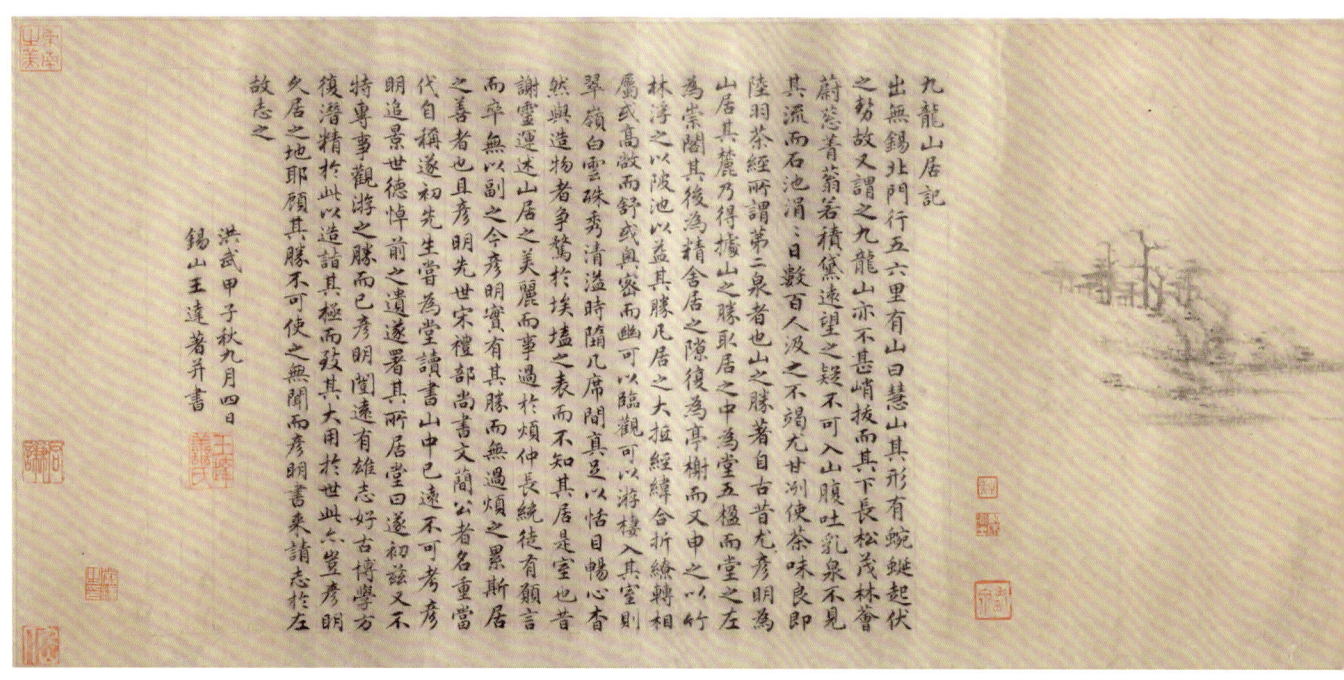

九龍山居記

出無錫北門行五六里有山曰慧山其形有蜿蜒起伏
之勢故文謂之九龍山亦不甚峭拔而其下長松茂林薈
蔚蒼菁菡蓞積黛遠望之疑不可入山腹吐乳泉不見
其流而石池湧之不竭凡汲之不涸九甘洌使茶味良即
陸羽茶經所謂第二泉者也山之勝者自昔尤著為
山居其麓乃得擴山之隙取居之中為堂五楹而堂之左
為崇閣其後為精舍居之隙復為亭榭而又申之以竹
林浮之以陂池以蓋其勝凡居之大抵經緯合折緣轉相
屬戍高敞而舒或真密而幽可以臨觀可以游樓入其室則
翠嶺白雲繞迷山居之美麗而事過於煩仲長統徳有顏言
然與造物者爭驚於塿塊之表而不知其居是室也昔
謝靈運述山居之美麗而事過於煩仲長統徳有顏言
而卒無以副之今彥明實有其勝而無過煩之累斯居
之善者也且彥明先世宋禮部尚書文簡公者名重當
代自稱遂初先生嘗為堂讀書山中已遠不可彥彥
明追景世德悼前之遺遂署其所居堂曰遂初誌又不
特專事觀游之勝而已彥明閒遠有雄志好古博學方
復潛精於此以造詣其極而致其大用於世此志堂又
久之地耶顧其勝不可使之無聞而彥明書來請志於左
故志之

洪武甲子秋九月四日
錫山王達善并書

### 51. 九龙山居图

元
（传）倪瓒
纸本设色
手卷
纵27.9、横146.1厘米
大都会艺术博物馆

### River Landscape with Thirteen Inscriptions

Yuan dynasty (1271–1368)
Attributed to Ni Zan
Ink and color on paper
Handscroll
H×W : 27.9×146.1 cm
The Metropolitan Museum of Art
Rogers Fund, 1918

不見倪迂今百年故山喬
木嶺蒼煙晴窗展卷
觀圖畫溪墨依然景
昔賢　吳郡唐寅

昔我游秦山㩦歌的春月尖兔
眉宇明涓苔虛首發蒼虬舞月
月來騎高彤彤僧之各持白雲
浣盡太湖出人煙美并梁溪寧
雲森此圖為渾此萄瑟嵯峨眼
中忽紛紛如伊梁甫呤君不見九
龍山凉一龍似
赤騎兩京八月余歸田童迢
慧山林野䉈酒宕山居晚出
書莊倪高士畫圖索顛拿不
知畫理因賦古體一章持後
南京刑部侍郎贈李少保
長洲顧應祥頓

芙蓉點：柳䅈：湖上秋風好
釣魚一鷗才堪當園士九龍山畫
入郊居雲來竹下偏肬酒且上
花間為䀹書欲賦遽初牘未可
近聞名蛀滿公卓
　　太原王穉登

共飛溪光蕩幽閣山影帶閒扉
披月朝烹澗寧雲畫采薇翹車
它日下巖數有光輝
　定靈子黃姬水書

諸伯雨鄙倪迂遠云孳畫
史鄉橫習壸求而有此帖
又不自鄙師子林爲云
非予畫生此如蒙閒迷吾
不至言自標置如此䫫此
信然
　　董其昌

百里梁溪曲岫嶢起薛蘿時春
雲水孤人少犯松過鳳史迴生
鼓龍丘隐翠阿世人遠望雲
只弓白雲島　義興馬治

莹尒清嫭地以人間望虛窗中
青霓禍愛蔓陈白雲島秋至瀟
叢桂春深長蘿薜漪沙玄
苾䒱荐荐蒞兰䒱 江浪陳壺牧

日暮空江寒遠渚記鴻起遙瞻吾友居
却在前山裏涼月淡疎林蒼煙接秋水
誰与會此情遊想雲林子
洪武丁卯夏五望日梁溪華　初武

宏朗孤生或據雲林山水永亭用眼為之
新經真堂一詞以淺之乎元季之善畫者
惟雲林仲圭賛文主林明子三壶畫圡
求名思為雲林之畫揚子鴻叔極
沈梅雅小谢而養宗龍為之一變七
親此古玄芙峡當時方俚母畫忘
習駒至志精冬能別士三䢛半

日雲萬壑雲嵐氣三客山六水活
葢朔玄渾遠青苕好古高燈弓
白雲嘉二緜雲儻几葉陈剛素
勢皇文囙古達達畫人空而梯
荶朴白練展　三橋之玄

高枕西神一草堂浮園雄揮翠
瀟颯青山至澗花千樹綠荃玄
亭草數行湖上時復鶴放門
前曲二九龍翔灡君自是裘
羊侣樂志道鈔擧仲長
茂苑文嘉

湖上山形趣九龍窟中秀色起三峯
堂在谷檀主貴勝已見周華子塁
散帳平麈延唇景横琴幽澗苔鳴
滨不知裘仲相過吾庭户長掃薛
荔封　止園居士閒玄城

山川互榮秀老屋翳煙蘿薴是
雲泉地今為松桂阿行邊飛鳥

## 52. 夏山隐居图 — Dwelling in Seclusion in Summer Mountains

元至正十四年（1354年）  
王蒙  
绢本设色  
立轴  
纵57.4、横34.5厘米  
弗利尔美术馆  

Yuan dynasty (1271–1368), dated 1354  
Wang Meng  
Ink and color on silk  
Hanging scroll  
H×W : 57.4×34.5 cm  
The Freer Gallery of Art  
Purchase–Charles Lang Freer Endowment

### 53. 林麓幽居图

元至正二十一年（1361年）
王蒙
纸本设色
立轴
纵177.8、横64.2厘米
芝加哥艺术博物馆

### Quiet Life in Wooded Glen

Yuan dynasty (1271–1368), dated 1361
Wang Meng
Ink and color on paper
Hanging scroll
H×W : 177.8×64.2 cm
The Art Institute of Chicago
Kate S. Buckingham Endowment Fund
© 2024. The Art Institute of Chicago / Art Resource, NY/ Scala, Florence

**54. 素庵图**

元
王蒙
纸本设色
立轴
纵136.5、横44.8厘米
大都会艺术博物馆

**Simple Retreat**

Yuan dynasty (1271–1368)
Wang Meng
Ink and color on paper
Hanging scroll
H×W : 136.5×44.8 cm
The Metropolitan Museum of Art
Ex coll.: C. C. Wang Family, Gift of Oscar L. Tang Family, 2012

### 55. 闭户著书图

元
王蒙
纸本设色
册页
纵66.7、横70.5厘米
克利夫兰艺术博物馆

**Writing Books Under Pine Trees**

Yuan dynasty (1271–1368)
Wang Meng
Ink and color on paper
Album leaf
H×W：66.7×70.5 cm
The Cleveland Museum of Art
Bequest of Mrs. A. Dean Perry 1997.94

#### 56. 丹崖翠壑图

元
（传）王蒙
纸本水墨
立轴
纵67.9、横34.3厘米
大都会艺术博物馆

#### Red Cliffs and Green Valleys

Yuan dynasty (1271–1368)
Attributed to Wang Meng
Ink on paper
Hanging scroll
H×W : 67.9×34.3 cm
The Metropolitan Museum of Art
Ex coll.: C. C. Wang Family, Purchase, Gift of Darius Ogden Mills and Gift of Mrs. Robert Young, by exchange, 1973

### 57. 九歌图

元至正二十一年（1361年）
张渥
纸本水墨
手卷
纵28、横438.2厘米
克利夫兰艺术博物馆

### Nine Songs

Yuan dynasty (1271–1368), dated 1361
Zhang Wo
Ink on paper
Handscroll
H×W : 28×438.2 cm
The Cleveland Museum of Art
Purchase from the J. H. Wade Fund 1959.138

## 58. 云山图

元
方从义
纸本设色
手卷
纵26.4、横144.8厘米
大都会艺术博物馆

## Cloudy Mountains

Yuan dynasty (1271–1368)

Fang Congyi

Ink and color on paper

Handscroll

H×W : 26.4×144.8 cm

The Metropolitan Museum of Art

Ex coll.: C. C. Wang Family, Purchase, Gift of J. Pierpont Morgan, by exchange, 1973

羽風流不歇到
羊何自詫道士
耽書換勝事爭
傳又好鵞

臣奢齡

傅聞東晉逸才多名士高風想
雅人深致靜中多此似溪梁
意若何解識山陰徽妙訣會心
宸賞幸如何至今能說山陰事鑒見
丹青寫換鵞
偶在一羣鷲

宣統庚申七月廿二日奉
勅敬題 臣鄭孝胥

筆墨精神少勝多廬叩

山蒼蒼水茫茫坡翁行彿
似瀟湘二十餘年
恐曾到耳聞漁父
雨鳴榔而乙見蛋悅
若夢伊誰憶此鷗
鷺心向時脫却
世塵應戴泊宅
李鼓枻乎瑞祥
雪坡道人

傳聞東晉逸才多名士高風想
永嘉周凱

方壺用筆多沙放難名重
如神澈綬林尕乐能尕此是卷箏
致淋漓頗得松雪筒神似外表興
艸明倣佛中苾芝勝趙元箏夾戊子冬
李逸大東月午攝姊婿慶所辭
己丑春正月吴湖帆假觀因日記

東圖用筆多沙及山固知彼居常所見
多淒草而涉俗者良非方
壺用意筆耳是卷上亭昕
藏蜀山圖同一精心可稱雙
壁並足以眣耀千古爲人世
昕希覯云
萬曆丁酉九月重九詹景鳳
東圖父識

雲山圖一幅上清高士方壺兩作也好事者藏之以為玩觀其筆法精到意態懇邃与米南宮高房山同一軌度非後來淺之為學者之此然而晴嵐曡嶂掩映於煙雲縹紗之際山坡一帯長景隱築巌岌然邃閣然無人盖仙家之勝境塵凡之絕觀也予家有方壺手淥一披其布置遠近大小錯陳不亂以優芳論鳴呼水墨之妙如方壺者不復多見矣其流落人間非一何餘七十載不能不使人重其景仰之思因為五言律一以紀其事云

不見瀛洲谷無聲意趣多斷雲迷
野墅遠樹帶山坡木容深潜跡樵人已罷歌投畜想高致清興欹無

正統十二年歲在丁卯夏後四月十有三日
工部右侍郎兼翰林院侍講學士
經筵官淮南高穀識

山中一雨塵氣萬塾千崖半是
雲石隱橫演清易見路穿深樹
杏難分參差樓觀仙侶逺迢
芝田下鶴摩何日移家来此住
春風龍上課耕耘
錢唐王諫

高人有造弹方壺塵氣盲
中华点无筆染雲煙藏造
化鞭驅龍虎捲江湖依稀
大海三洲境仿佛長江萬里
圖楊氏珎藏宜世守而題展
玩屬吾徒
吳郡沈成章

絕境非凡境蓬萊
咫尺間深林茅屋静
流水野橋閑天迥鳥
飛後山空雲自還地
偏人跡少松徑雨苔
斑
雲間錢博

一序臨河歲月多茂林脩竹
近如何却欣觀察都成逰當
日興懷不獨羲

### 59. 风雨归舟图

元
方从义
纸本设色
立轴
纵46.6、横43.3厘米
克利夫兰艺术博物馆

### Landscape Ink-play

Yuan dynasty (1271–1368)
Fang Congyi
Ink and color on paper
Hanging scroll
H×W : 46.6×43.3 cm
The Cleveland Museum of Art
John L. Severance Fund 1982.34

### 60. 罗浮山樵图

元至正二十六年（1366年）
陈汝言
绢本水墨
立轴
纵107、横54厘米
克利夫兰艺术博物馆

### Woodcutter of Mount Luofu

Yuan dynasty (1271–1368), dated 1366
Chen Ruyan
Ink on silk
Hanging scroll
H×W : 107×54 cm
The Cleveland Museum of Art
Gift of Mrs. A. Dean Perry 1964.156

### 61. 仙山楼阁图

元
陈汝言
绢本设色
手卷
纵33.5、横98厘米
克利夫兰艺术博物馆

### Mountains of Immortals

Yuan dynasty (1271–1368)
Chen Ruyan
Ink and color on silk
Handscroll
H×W : 33.5×98 cm
The Cleveland Museum of Art
Bequest of Mrs. A. Dean Perry 1997.95

錢惟善江月松風集有題廣徵天師畫
龍圖詩曰噓氣乘雲搏太清卷卻靈怪
硯池腥波濤光彩失雙鯢風雨暝冥六
丁朱火騰空超碧落翠鱗垂水捲洛溪
真人上挾飛仙去安得攀髯過洞庭

嘉慶丙子二月五日　　　　　　成親王 錄

## 62. 霖雨图

元
张羽材
绢本水墨
手卷
纵26.8、横271.8厘米
大都会艺术博物馆

## Beneficent Rain

Yuan dynasty (1271–1368)
Zhang Yucai
Ink on silk
Handscroll
H×W : 26.8×271.8 cm
The Metropolitan Museum of Art
Gift of Douglas Dillon, 1985

## 63. 牧牛图 — Herd Boys and Buffalo in Landscape

| | |
|---|---|
| 元 | Yuan dynasty (1271–1368) |
| 郭敏 | Guo Min |
| 绢本水墨 | Ink on silk |
| 立轴 | Hanging scroll |
| 纵92、横56.5厘米 | H×W : 92×56.5 cm |
| 克利夫兰艺术博物馆 | The Cleveland Museum of Art |
| | John L. Severance Fund 1999.216.1 |

**64. 绿竹清幽图**

元至正二年（1342年）
王渊
绢本设色
立轴
纵211、横95厘米
普林斯顿大学美术馆

**Pure Serenity of Green Bamboo**

Yuan dynasty (1271–1368), dated 1342
Wang Yuan
Ink and color on silk
Hanging scroll
H×W : 211×95 cm
The Princeton University Art Museum
Gift of DuBois Schanck Morris, Class of 1893
© 2024. Princeton University Art Museum/Art Resource NY/Scala, Florence

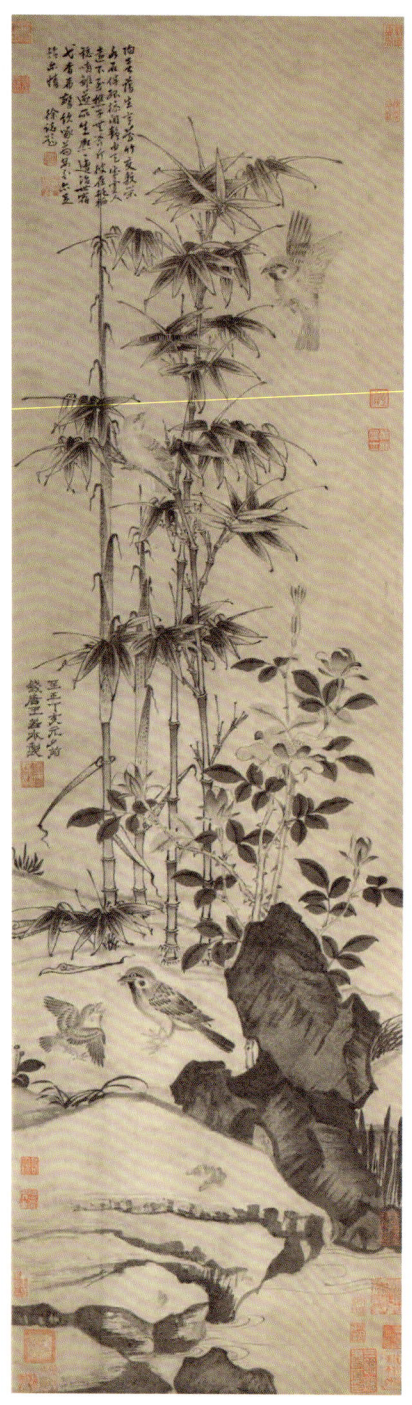

### 65. 花竹山禽图

元至正七年（1347年）
王渊
纸本水墨
立轴
纵116.84、横33.02厘米
印第安纳波利斯艺术博物馆

### Bamboo, Sparrows and Camellias

Yuan dynasty (1271–1368), dated 1347
Wang Yuan
Ink on paper
Hanging scroll
H×W : 116.84×33.02 cm
The Indianapolis Museum of Art
Gift of Mr. and Mrs. Eli Lilly

### 66. 秋景鹑雀图

元至正七年（1347年）
王渊
纸本水墨
立轴
纵114.3、横56厘米
克利夫兰艺术博物馆

### Quails and Sparrows in Autumn Scene

Yuan dynasty (1271–1368), dated 1347
Wang Yuan
Ink on paper
Hanging scroll
H×W : 114.3×56 cm
The Cleveland Museum of Art
Bequest of Mrs. A. Dean Perry 1997.91

### 67. 竹雀图

元
（传）王渊
纸本水墨
立轴
纵139.3、横49.9厘米
大阪市立美术馆

### Bamboo and Sparrows

Yuan dynasty (1271–1368)
Attributed to Wang Yuan
Ink on paper
Hanging scroll
H×W : 139.3×49.9 cm
The Osaka City Museum of Fine Arts

### 68. 磐石云林图

元
张逊
绢本水墨
立轴
纵90.8、横42.5厘米
大都会艺术博物馆

### Rocky Landscape with Pines

Yuan dynasty (1271–1368)
Zhang Xun
Ink on silk
Hanging scroll
H×W : 90.8×42.5 cm
The Metropolitan Museum of Art
Ex coll.: C. C. Wang Family, Gift of Oscar L. Tang Family, 2008

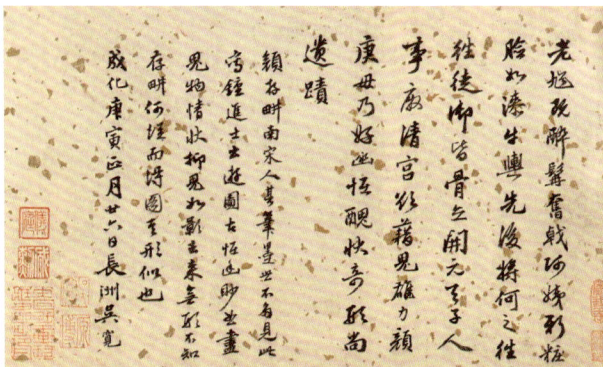

### 69. 钟馗嫁妹图 — Demon Queller Zhong Kui Giving His Sister Away in Marriage

元
（传）颜庚
绢本水墨
手卷
纵24.4、横253.4厘米
大都会艺术博物馆

Yuan dynasty (1271–1368)
Attributed to Yan Geng
Ink on silk
Handscroll
H×W : 24.4×253.4 cm
The Metropolitan Museum of Art
Purchase, The Dillon Fund Gift and Rogers Fund, 1990

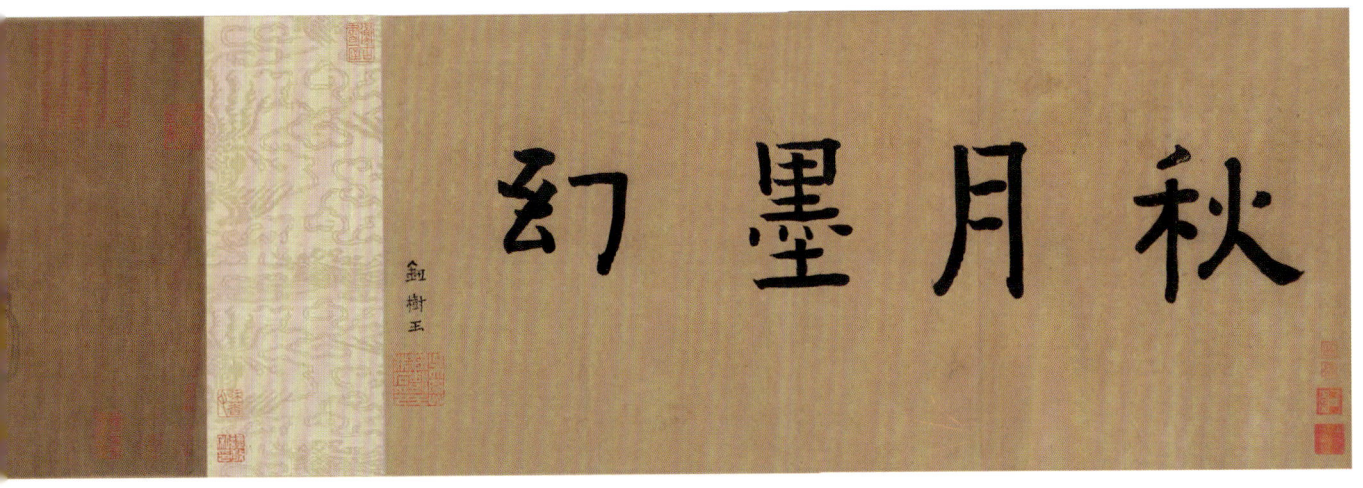

### 70. 钟馗元夜出游图     Lantern Night Excursion of Zhong Kui

元  
颜辉  
绢本设色  
手卷  
纵24.8、横240.3厘米  
克利夫兰艺术博物馆

Yuan dynasty (1271–1368)  
Yan Hui  
Ink and color on silk  
Handscroll  
H×W : 24.8×240.3 cm  
The Cleveland Museum of Art  
Mr. and Mrs. William H. Marlatt Fund 1961.206

### 71. 寒山拾得图    Hanshan and Shide

元  
（传）颜辉  
绢本设色  
立轴  
每联：纵127.6、横41.8厘米  
东京国立博物馆

Yuan dynasty (1271–1368)  
Attributed to Yan Hui  
Ink and color on silk  
Hanging scroll  
H×W(each scroll) : 127.6×41.8 cm  
The Tokyo National Museum  
ColBase（https://colbase.nich.go.jp/collection_items/tnm/TA-148?locale=ja）

**72. 月梅图**

元
（传）颜辉
绢本水墨
册页
纵26、横28.3厘米
克利夫兰艺术博物馆

**Plum Blossoms in Moonlight**

Yuan dynasty (1271–1368)
Attributed to Yan Hui
Ink on silk
Album leaf
H×W : 26×28.3 cm
The Cleveland Museum of Art
Andrew R. and Martha Holden Jennings
Fund 1978.49

## 73. 五祖再来图

元
因陀罗
纸本水墨
立轴
纵32.7、横44.6厘米
克利夫兰艺术博物馆

## Second Coming of Fifth Patriarch

Yuan dynasty (1271–1368)
Yintuoluo
Ink on paper
Hanging scroll
H×W : 32.7×44.6 cm
The Cleveland Museum of Art
Purchase from the J. H. Wade Fund 1967.211

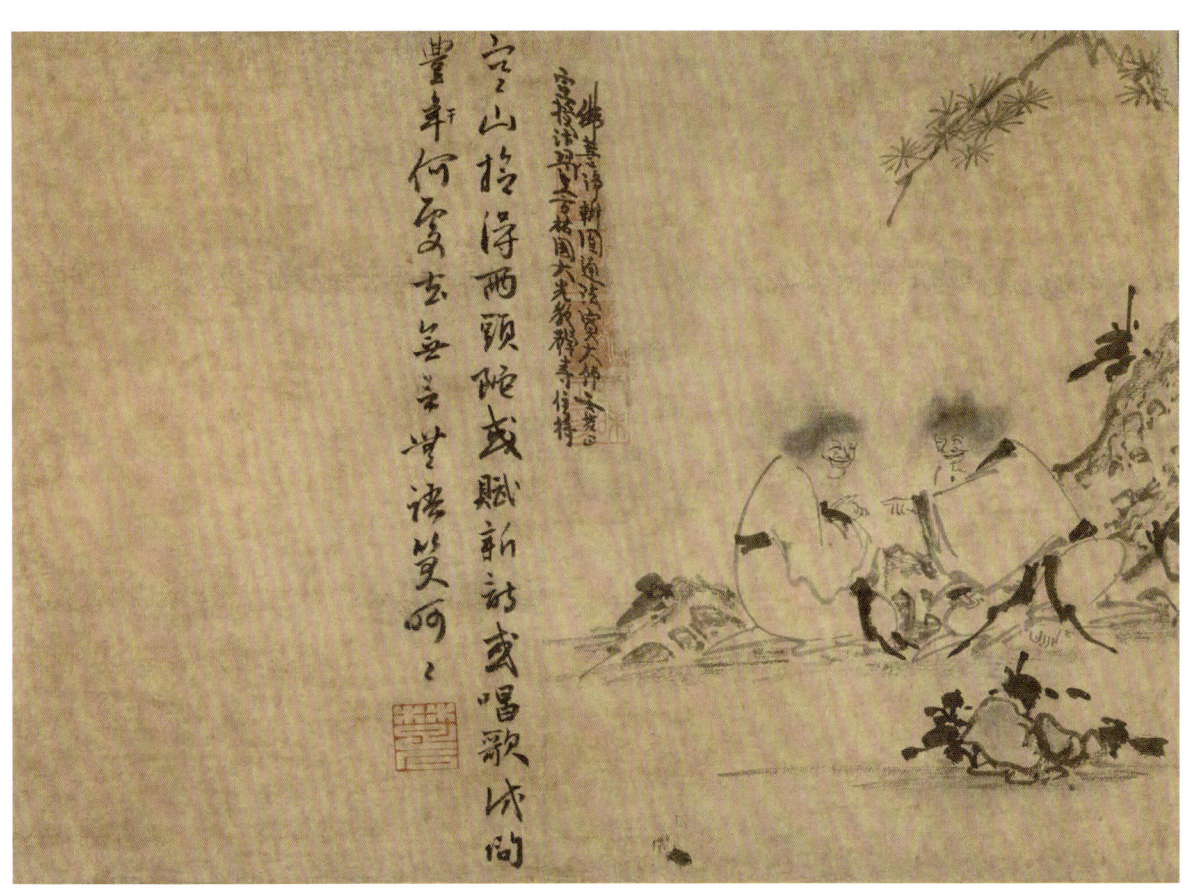

### 74. 寒山拾得图

元
因陀罗
绢本水墨
立轴
纵35、横49.5厘米
东京国立博物馆

### Hanshan and Shide

Yuan dynasty (1271–1368)
Yintuoluo
Ink on silk
Hanging scroll
H×W : 35×49.5 cm
The Tokyo National Museum
ColBase（https://colbase.nich.go.jp/collection_items/tnm/TA-343?locale=ja）

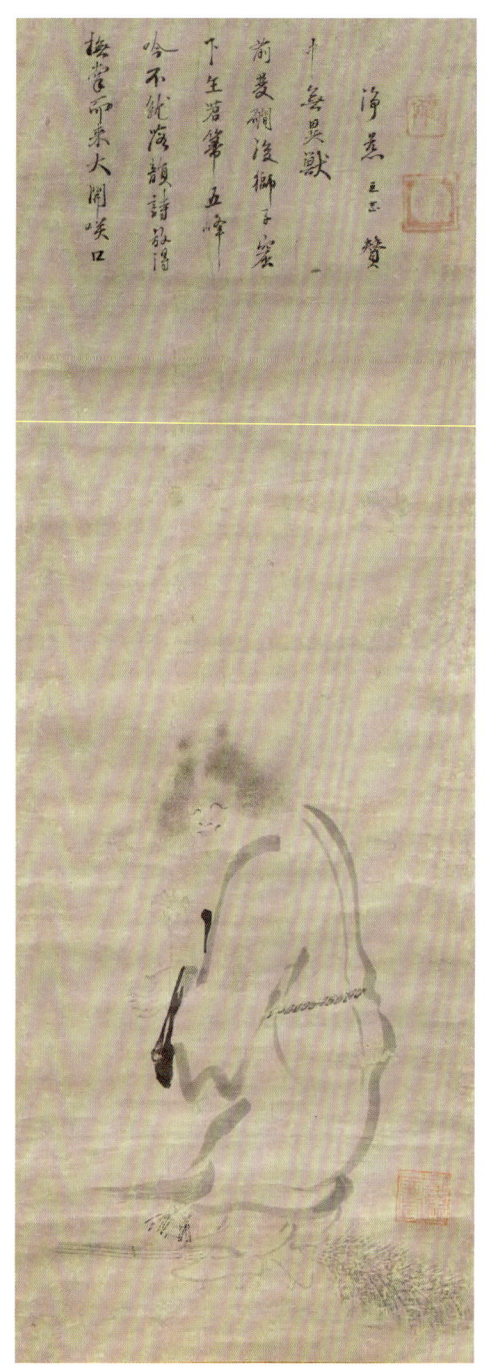

### 75. 拾得图

元
（传）因陀罗
纸本水墨
立轴
纵87.5、横31.2厘米
耶鲁大学艺术博物馆

### Shide

Yuan dynasty (1271–1368)
Attributed to Yintuoluo
Ink on paper
Hanging scroll
H×W : 87.5×31.2 cm
The Yale University Art Gallery
Mary Griggs Burke Collection, Gift of the Mary and Jackson Burke Foundation

**76. 达摩渡江图**

元
（传）李尧夫
纸本水墨
立轴
纵85.7、横33.8厘米
大都会艺术博物馆

**Bodhidharma Crossing Yangzi River on Reed**

Yuan dynasty (1271–1368)
Attributed to Li Yaofu
Ink on paper
Hanging scroll
H×W : 85.7×33.8 cm
The Metropolitan Museum of Art
Edward Elliott Family Collection, Purchase, The Dillon Fund Gift, 1982

吳餘慶字彥積號斯亨宜黃人能
詩文永樂六年薦除中書舍人歷
在通政兼知制誥論者謂其小楷
書如美女簪花大草如瑞雲飛空
流水赴壑 佩文齋書畫譜

紫賁經鋤厚貺法爺紙本真迹卷子其樹在絕巘曾
雲出徐幼文人物則任月山巓秋月堪與同語元人中上
乘也吳斯白梧蕃心經東流麗東深嚴自楷門內陰西
斫銳米山元人仕明者春篇蔵陛小徐便廬尚馬家傳
是徒道物也己巳六月待于吳門帆舡下栖影萬年
近見清内府舊蔵元人九卷 趙善長林之奐画節
用筆亦祠穆沈厚與紫賁相伯仲在房山子
久之後盖亦風雨使然否 醜簃文識 長軒眼福
辛卯十月八日試

近於歲中覓阿陽畫所謂
篆法如雲長仿佛見其六字
迎象久之至懷不能也頃得
升卷宛然鄭畫宋元相
去其不遠乎 壬申夏愷郷

渤海生李升識

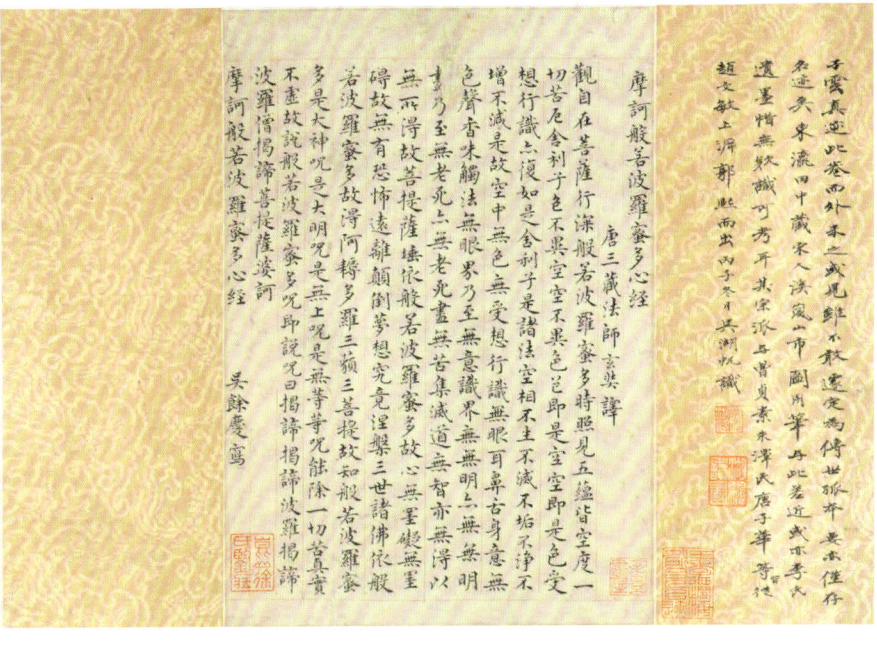

### 77. 佛渡五比丘图

元
李升
纸本水墨
手卷
纵26.7、横110.5厘米
克利夫兰艺术博物馆

### Buddha's Convertion of Five Bhiksu

Yuan dynasty (1271–1368)
Li Sheng
Ink on paper
Handscroll
H×W : 26.7×110.5 cm
The Cleveland Museum of Art
Bequest of Mrs. A. Dean Perry 1997.92

## 78. 刘晨阮肇入天台山图

元
赵苍云
纸本水墨
手卷
纵22.5、横564厘米
大都会艺术博物馆

## Liu Chen and Ruan Zhao Entering Tiantai Mountains

Yuan dynasty (1271–1368)
Zhao Cangyun
Ink on paper
Handscroll
H×W : 22.5×564 cm
The Metropolitan Museum of Art
Ex coll.: C. C. Wang Family, Gift of Oscar L. Tang Family, 2005

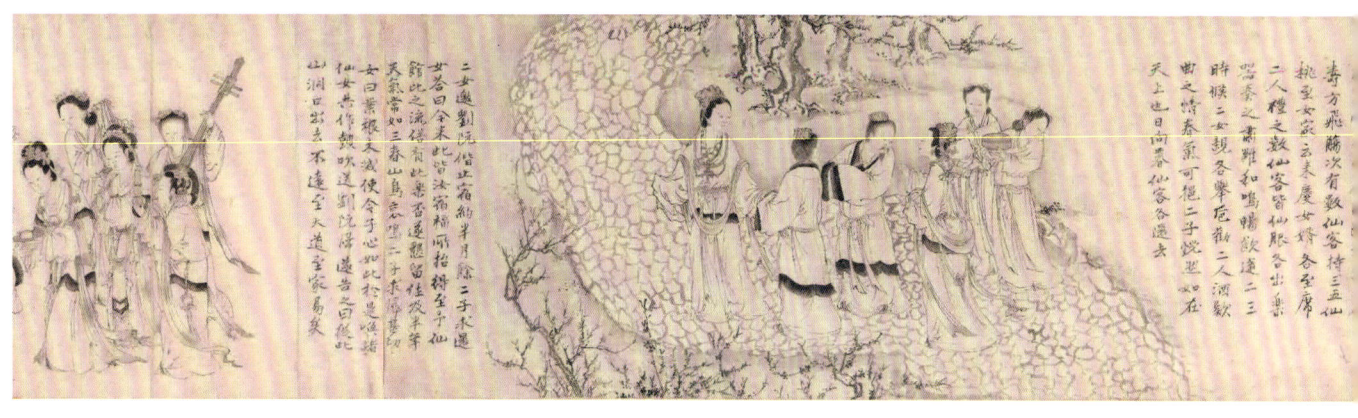

壽方飛騰次有數仙客持三五仙
桃至女家云來慶女婿各至席
二人禮之教仙客皆仙眷各出果
餚秦之音難和鳴暢歐歌三
時撲二女親各舉巵勸二人酒歡
曲之時春氣可悒二人悅起以在
天上也日向暮仙家各過去

二女邀劉阮偕止宿約半月除二子求還
女答曰余未此皆汝宿福所招携至子仙
館此之流徒有此法若更還留佳哎半年
天氣常如三春山鳥之聲二子悲嘆請
女曰罪根太滅使余于心恐松恩嘆諸
仙女無不作敢吹送劉阮歸邊告以歸
山洞曰汝去不遠至大道宝家馬矣

劉阮洞中遇仙人
天和樹色霽濛濛霞重嵐溪
劉阮茫雲寶寶滿山無鳥雀水
檣江澗有笙簧碧沙洞裡乾
坤別紅樹枝邊日月長頻滿花
間有人出免令仙犬吠劉郎
仙人送劉阮出洞
殷勤相送出天台仙境那能卻
再來雲液既歸須強飲玉書無
事莫頻開花當洞口應長在不
別人間空不迴悵悵瀛顏徒此別
碧山明月照蒼苔
　　宋芭

蒼雲山八木道宋崇寧萬壽寺僧繪事入神山
水横秋夫都似沒有圖而生動過之人物工細別有
姿韻世不多見所作劉阮天台舊盤蕭散神趣
間遠書表天帶設色妍妙及所作嘉眷安外物表之趣
偶示道菩容玉孫天台員人郄桌為荒矣有
劉院本呆非義有子慶后人宦像妹心展甚恣仙清
情投嬌竊有猶枝氏事作俺中強其後子作奧西南此人
未看林潤仿拂祿市無從躁踽世人污其外塊妻申
清風紅門追蒼雲甲微郎在厷念名在年午园上下燃水帘
洪武十二年秋九月華初武書於春卅軒
　　　　　　　　道行識

千　　　　　　　蒼雲山人畫書

二子出洞口行至大道回首惟桃花爛熳谿山色依舊而已甫至家纔無相識纔纔里雄異乃聞得七代子孫傳上祖入山不出不知今何在

烟霭氤氲的是迷离梦境 杨重英山斋父识

## 79. 司马才仲梦苏小小图 — Sima Caizhong's Dream of Courtesan, Su Xiaoxiao

金
(传) 刘元
绢本设色
手卷
尺寸不详
辛辛那提艺术博物馆

Jin dynasty (1115–1234)
Attributed to Liu Yuan
Ink and color on silk
Handscroll
Dimensions unknown
The Cincinnati Art Museum
J. J. Emery Endowment and Fanny Bryce Lehmer Endowment
© Bridgeman Images

**80. 麻姑献寿图**

元
（传）陈月溪
绢本设色
立轴
纵102.5、横54.5厘米
波士顿艺术博物馆

**Daoist Immortal Magu with Crane and Flower Basket**

Yuan dynasty (1271–1368)
Attributed to Chen Yuexi
Ink and color on silk
Hanging scroll
H×W : 102.5×54.5 cm
The Museum of Fine Arts, Boston
William Sturgis Bigelow Collection
© 2024 Museum of Fine Arts, Boston

**81. 松鼠栗树图**

元
（传）葛淑英
纸本水墨
立轴
纵97、横39.4厘米
克利夫兰艺术博物馆

**Squirrels on Chestnut Tree**

Yuan dynasty (1271–1368)
Attributed to Ge Shuying
Ink on paper
Hanging scroll
H×W : 97×39.4 cm
The Cleveland Museum of Art
John L. Severance Fund 1979.70

## 82. 丹枫双鸟图

元
（传）郑禧
绢本设色
立轴
纵73.66、横40.64厘米
印第安纳波利斯艺术博物馆

## Two Birds on Red Maple

Yuan dynasty (1271–1368)
Attributed to Zheng Xi
Ink and color on silk
Hanging scroll
H×W : 73.66×40.64 cm
The Indianapolis Museum of Art
Gift of James W. Alsdorf

## 83. 孔雀芙蓉图

元
（传）边鲁
绢本设色
立轴
纵169.9、横102.2厘米
大都会艺术博物馆

## Peahen and Hibiscus

Yuan dynasty (1271–1368)
Attributed to Bian Lu
Ink and color on silk
Hanging scroll
H×W : 169.9×102.2 cm
The Metropolitan Museum of Art
Purchase, The Dillon Fund and The B. Y. Lam Foundation Gifts, 1995

## 84. 石竹图

元
（传）檀芝瑞
纸本水墨
立轴
纵100.3、横38厘米
金贝尔艺术博物馆

## Bamboo and Rocks

Yuan dynasty (1271–1368)
Attributed to Tan Zhirui
Ink on paper
Hanging scroll
H×W : 100.3×38 cm
The Kimbell Art Museum
Kimbell Art Museum, Fort Worth, Texas.
AP 2002.02

**85. 山水图**

元
（传）檀芝瑞
绢本水墨
立轴
纵39.6、横23.9厘米
荷兰国立博物馆

**Bamboo Forest at Night**

Yuan dynasty (1271–1368)
Attributed to Tan Zhirui
Ink on silk
Hanging scroll
H×W : 39.6×23.9 cm
The Rijksmuseum
On loan from the Royal Asian Art Society in The Netherlands (gift of Carolina Geertruida Verburgt–Kramers, 1955)

### 86. 风竹图

元
普明
绢本水墨
立轴
纵78、横46厘米
克利夫兰艺术博物馆

### Bamboo in Wind

Yuan dynasty (1271–1368)
Puming
Ink on silk
Hanging scroll
H×W : 78×46 cm
The Cleveland Museum of Art
John L. Severance Fund 1953.246

**87. 竹石图**

元
邓宇
纸本水墨
立轴
纵135.1、横42.2厘米
大都会艺术博物馆

**Bamboo and Rock**

Yuan dynasty (1271–1368)
Deng Yu
Ink on paper
Hanging scroll
H×W : 135.1×42.2 cm
The Metropolitan Museum of Art
From the P. Y. and Kinmay W. Tang Family Collection, Gift of Oscar L. Tang, 1991

## 88. 水墨花卉图

元至正二十一年（1361年）
赵衷
纸本水墨
手卷
纵31.8、横153.2厘米
克利夫兰艺术博物馆

## Ink Flowers

Yuan dynasty (1271–1368), dated 1361
Zhao Zhong
Ink on paper
Handscroll
H×W : 31.8×153.2 cm
The Cleveland Museum of Art
John L. Severance Fund 1967.36

**89. 河蟹图**

元
（传）卫九鼎
绢本水墨
册页
纵23.5、横31.7厘米
波士顿艺术博物馆

**River Crab**

Yuan dynasty (1271–1368)
Attributed to Wei Jiuding
Ink on silk
Alumb Leaf
H×W : 23.5×31.7 cm
The Museum of Fine Arts, Boston
Keith McLeod Fund
© 2024 Museum of Fine Arts, Boston

## 90. 萱蝶图

元
刘善守
绢本水墨
立轴
纵160、横58.4厘米
克利夫兰艺术博物馆

## Lily and Butterflies

Yuan dynasty (1271–1368)
Liu Shanshou
Ink on silk
Hanging scroll
H×W : 160×58.4 cm
The Cleveland Museum of Art
Purchase from the J. H. Wade Fund 1971.132

## 91. 龙松图    Dragon Pine

元或明  
吴伯理  
纸本水墨  
立轴  
纵121.9、横33.7厘米  
大都会艺术博物馆

Yuan dynasty (1271–1368) or Ming dynasty (1368–1644)  
Wu Boli  
Ink on paper  
Hanging scroll  
H×W : 121.9×33.7 cm  
The Metropolitan Museum of Art  
Edward Elliott Family Collection, Gift of Douglas Dillon, 1984

**92. 澄溪静樾图**

元
马琬
纸本水墨
立轴
尺寸不详
辛辛那提艺术博物馆

**Quiet River at Foot of Misty Mountains**

Yuan dynasty (1271–1368)
Ma Wan
Ink on paper
Hanging scroll
Dimensions unknown
The Cincinnati Art Museum
John J. Emery Endowment and Fanny Bryce Lehmer Endowment
© Bridgeman Images

### 93. 丹台春晓图

元
陆广
纸本水墨
立轴
纵61.6、横26厘米
大都会艺术博物馆

### Spring Dawn over Elixir Terrace

Yuan dynasty (1271–1368)
Lu Guang
Ink on paper
Hanging scroll
H×W : 61.6×26 cm
The Metropolitan Museum of Art
Ex coll.: C. C. Wang Family, Edward Elliott Family Collection, Purchase, The Dillon Fund Gift, 1982

**94. 雪景山水图**

元
孙君泽
绢本设色
立轴
纵126、横56.5厘米
东京国立博物馆

**Snowscape**

Yuan dynasty (1271–1368)
Sun Junze
Ink and color on silk
Hanging scroll
H×W : 126×56.5 cm
The Tokyo National Museum
ColBase（https://colbase.nich.go.jp/collection_items/tnm/TA-141?locale=ja）

**95. 竹居图**

元
（传）孙君泽
绢本水墨
立轴
纵117、横30厘米
集美博物馆

**Landscape Under Bamboo**

Yuan dynasty (1271–1368)
Attributed to Sun Junze
Ink on silk
Hanging scroll
H×W : 117×30 cm
The Guimet Museum
© RMN–Grand Palais (MNAAG, Paris) / Thierry Ollivier

**96. 雪中双鹿图**

元
周渊
绢本设色
立轴
纵179.7、横92.4厘米
弗利尔美术馆

**Stag, Doe and Red Camellias in Snow**

Yuan dynasty (1271–1368)
Zhou Yuan
Ink and color on silk
Hanging scroll
H×W : 179.7×92.4 cm
The Freer Gallery of Art
Gift of Charles Lang Freer

**97. 华严三圣图**

**Sakyamuni Triad: Buddha Attended by Manjusri and Samantabhadra**

元
佚名
绢本设色
立轴
每联：纵106.9、横46.4厘米
克利夫兰艺术博物馆

Yuan dynasty (1271–1368)
Artist unknown
Ink and color on silk
Hanging scroll
H×W (each scroll) : 106.9×46.4 cm
The Cleveland Museum of Art
Purchase from the J. H. Wade Fund 2009.342

## 98. 如来像

元
佚名
绢本设色
立轴
纵100.4、横37厘米
波士顿艺术博物馆

## Buddha

Yuan dynasty (1271–1368)
Artist unknown
Ink and color on silk
Hanging scroll
H×W : 100.4×37 cm
The Museum of Fine Arts, Boston
Denman Waldo Ross Collection
© 2024 Museum of Fine Arts, Boston

**99. 释迦牟尼像**

元
佚名
绢本设色
立轴
纵96.8、横45.7厘米
克利夫兰艺术博物馆

**Sakyamuni Buddha**

Yuan dynasty (1271–1368)
Artist unknown
Ink and color on silk
Hanging scroll
H×W : 96.8×45.7 cm
The Cleveland Museum of Art
John L. Severance Fund 1987.75

**100. 孔雀明王像**

辽
佚名
布本设色
立轴
纵141.4、横88.3厘米
芝加哥艺术博物馆

**Mahamayuri Vidyaraja**

Liao dynasty (907–1125)
Artist unknown
Ink and color on cotton
Hanging scroll
H×W : 141.4×88.3 cm
The Art Institute of Chicago
Kate S. Buckingham Endowment
© 2024. The Art Institute of Chicago / Art Resource, NY/ Scala, Florence

### 101. 元照律师大智像

金
佚名
绢本设色
立轴
纵92.4、横40.5厘米
克利夫兰艺术博物馆

### Portrait of Priest Dazhi Master of Law

Jin dynasty (1115–1234)
Artist unknown
Ink and color on silk
Hanging scroll
H×W : 92.4×40.5 cm
The Cleveland Museum of Art
Purchase from the J. H. Wade Fund 1974.29

**102. 罗汉像**

元
佚名
绢本设色
立轴
纵112.4、横49.1厘米
大都会艺术博物馆

**Arhat**

Yuan dynasty (1271–1368)
Artist unknown
Ink and color on silk
Hanging scroll
H×W : 112.4×49.1 cm
The Metropolitan Museum of Art
Purchase, Seymour Fund and Bequest of
Dorothy Graham Bennett, 1984

## 103. 罗汉图一

元或明
佚名
绢本设色
立轴
纵125.7、横67厘米
波士顿艺术博物馆

**Arhats**

Yuan dynasty (1271–1368) or Ming dynasty (1368–1644)
Artist unknown
Ink and color on silk
Hanging scroll
H×W : 125.7×67 cm
The Museum of Fine Arts, Boston
Julia Bradford Huntington James Fund
© 2024 Museum of Fine Arts, Boston

## 104. 罗汉图二

元
佚名
绢本设色
立轴
纵125.7、横67.1厘米
波士顿艺术博物馆

## Arhats

Yuan dynasty (1271–1368)
Artist unknown
Ink and color on silk
Hanging scroll
H×W : 125.7×67.1 cm
The Museum of Fine Arts, Boston
Julia Bradford Huntington James Fund
© 2024 Museum of Fine Arts, Boston

### 105. 罗汉像

元至正五年（1345年）
佚名
绢本设色
立轴
纵128、横62.2厘米
大都会艺术博物馆

### Arhat

Yuan dynasty (1271–1368), dated 1345
Artist unknown
Ink and color on silk
Hanging scroll
H×W : 128×62.2 cm
The Metropolitan Museum of Art
From the Collection of A. W. Bahr, Purchase, Fletcher Fund, 1947

## 106. 罗汉像

元至正五年（1345年）
佚名
绢本设色
立轴
纵126.2、横62.6厘米
弗利尔美术馆

## Arhat

Yuan dynasty (1271–1368), dated 1345
Artist unknown
Ink and color on silk
Hanging scroll
H×W : 126.2×62.6 cm
The Freer Gallery of Art
Gift of Ruth Meyer Epstein

## 107. 罗汉像

元至正五年（1345年）
佚名
绢本设色
立轴
纵125.6、横62.2厘米
弗利尔美术馆

## Arhat

Yuan dynasty (1271–1368), dated 1345
Artist unknown
Ink and color on silk
Hanging scroll
H×W : 125.6×62.2 cm
The Freer Gallery of Art
Bequest of Mrs. Katharine Graham

**108. 罗汉图**

元
佚名
绢本设色
立轴
纵148.4、横76.6厘米
弗利尔美术馆

**Arhat**

Yuan dynasty (1271–1368)
Artist unknown
Ink and color on silk
Hanging scroll
H×W : 148.4×76.6 cm
The Freer Gallery of Art
Gift of Charles Lang Freer

### 109. 二仙像 — Daoist Immortals

元或明  
佚名  
绢本水墨  
立轴  
纵96.52、横40.64厘米  
印第安纳波利斯艺术博物馆  

Yuan dynasty (1271–1368) or Ming dynasty (1368–1644)  
Artist unknown  
Ink on silk  
Hanging scroll  
H×W : 96.52×40.64 cm  
The Indianapolis Museum of Art  
Gift of Mr. and Mrs. Ben Domont and son, Dan Domont

### 110. 铁拐李像

元或明
佚名
绢本设色
立轴
纵107、横38.5厘米
克利夫兰艺术博物馆

### Immortal Li Tieguai

Yuan dynasty (1271–1368) or Ming dynasty (1368–1644)
Artist unknown
Ink and color on silk
Hanging scroll
H×W : 107×38.5 cm
The Cleveland Museum of Art
Edward L. Whittemore Fund 1982.29.1

## 111. 刘海戏蟾图

元
佚名
绢本设色
立轴
纵105、横38厘米
克利夫兰艺术博物馆

## Immortal Liu Haichan

Yuan dynasty (1271–1368)
Artist unknown
Ink and color on silk
Hanging scroll
H×W : 105×38 cm
The Cleveland Museum of Art
Edward L. Whittemore Fund 1982.29.2

### 112. 达摩苇渡江图

元
佚名
纸本水墨
立轴
纵175、横38.5厘米
克利夫兰艺术博物馆

### Bodhidharma Crossing Yangzi on Reed

Yuan dynasty (1271–1368)
Artist unknown
Ink on paper
Hanging scroll
H×W : 175×38.5 cm
The Cleveland Museum of Art
John L. Severance Fund 1964.44

**113. 寒山拾得图**    **Hanshan and Shide**

元或明  Yuan dynasty (1271–1368) or Ming dynasty (1368–1644)
佚名  Artist unknown
绢本设色  Ink and color on silk
立轴  Hanging scroll
纵127、横51.2厘米  H×W：127×51.2 cm
波士顿艺术博物馆  The Museum of Fine Arts, Boston
Bequest of Charles Bain Hoyt–Charles Bain Hoyt Collection
© 2024 Museum of Fine Arts, Boston

**114. 元人饮马图**

元或明
佚名
绢本设色
立轴
纵169.5、横101厘米
集美博物馆

**Horse Stop and Mongolian Horsemen**

Yuan dynasty (1271–1368) or Ming dynasty (1368–1644)
Artist unknown
Ink and color on silk
Hanging scroll
H×W : 169.5×101 cm
The Guimet Museum
© RMN–Grand Palais (MNAAG, Paris) / Thierry Ollivier

### 115. 人马图

元或明
佚名
绢本设色
册页
纵28、横29.2厘米
耶鲁大学艺术博物馆

### Horse and Groom

Yuan dynasty (1271–1368) or Ming dynasty (1368–1644)
Aritist unknown
Ink and color on silk
Album leaf
H×W : 28×29.2 cm
Yale University Art Gallery
Hobart and Edward Small Moore Memorial Collection,
Bequest of Mrs. William H. Moore

**116. 蹴鞠图**

元或明
佚名
绢本设色
立轴
纵115.6、横55.3厘米
克利夫兰美术馆

**Football Players**

Yuan dynasty (1271–1368) or Ming dynasty (1368–1644)
Aritist unknown
Ink and color on silk
Hanging scroll
H×W : 115.6×55.3 cm
The Cleveland Museum of Art
Gift of Mr. and Mrs. Wilbur Cowett 1971.26

**117. 竹林仕女图**

元
佚名
绢本设色
册页
纵22.86、横22.23厘米
耶鲁大学艺术博物馆

**Lady Among Bamboo and Plum**

Yuan dynasty (1271–1368)
Artist unknown
Ink and color on silk
Album leaf
H×W : 22.86×22.23 cm
The Yale University Art Gallery
Hobart and Edward Small Moore Memorial
Collection, Gift of Mrs. William H. Moore

### 118. 寒山拾得图

元或明
佚名
纸本水墨
立轴
纵27.3、横13厘米
耶鲁大学艺术博物馆

### Hanshan and Shide

Yuan dynasty (1271–1368) or Ming dynasty (1368–1644)
Aritist unknown
Ink on paper
Hanging scroll
H×W : 27.3×13 cm
The Yale University Art Gallery
Hobart and Edward Small Moore Memorial
Collection, Gift of Mrs. William H. Moore

### 119. 牧羊图 — Sheep and Herd Boy

| | |
|---|---|
| 元或明 | Yuan dynasty (1271–1368) or Ming dynasty (1368–1644) |
| 佚名 | Artist unknown |
| 绢本设色 | Ink and color on silk |
| 册页 | Album leaf |
| 纵24.1、横24.8厘米 | H×W : 24.1×24.8 cm |
| 大都会艺术博物馆 | The Metropolitan Museum of Art |
| | John Stewart Kennedy Fund, 1913 |

### 120. 携琴访隐图

元或明
佚名
绢本设色
立轴
纵177.17、横60.48厘米
明尼阿波利斯美术馆

### Visiting Recluse with Qin

Yuan dynasty (1271–1368) or Ming dynasty (1368–1644)
Aritist unknown
Ink and color on silk
Hanging scroll
H×W : 177.17×60.48 cm
The Minneapolis Institute of Art
The Friends of Bruce Dayton Art Acquisition Fund

**121. 货郎图**

| | **Sweetmeat Vendor and Child** |
|---|---|
| 元或明 | Yuan dynasty (1271–1368) or Ming dynasty (1368–1644) |
| 佚名 | Artist unknown |
| 绢本设色 | Ink and color on silk |
| 立轴 | Hanging scroll |
| 纵101.4、横66.3厘米 | H×W : 101.4×66.3 cm |
| 波士顿艺术博物馆 | The Museum of Fine Arts, Boston |
| | Bequest of Charles Bain Hoyt—Charles Bain Hoyt Collection |
| | © 2024 Museum of Fine Arts, Boston |

### 122. 宫殿图

元或明
佚名
绢本设色
册页
直径：26.2 厘米
克利夫兰艺术博物馆

### Palace

Yuan dynasty (1271–1368) or Ming dynasty (1368–1644)
Artist unknown
Ink and color on silk
Album leaf
Diameter: 26.2 cm
The Cleveland Museum of Art
Gift of the John Huntington Art and Polytechnic Trust
1915.704

### 123. 牧牛图 — Oxen

元或明 — Yuan dynasty (1271–1368) or Ming dynasty (1368–1644)
佚名 — Artist unknown
绢本水墨 — Ink on silk
手卷 — Handscroll
尺寸不详 — Dimensions unknownn
不列颠博物馆 — The British Museum
Purchased from: George Eumorfopoulos
© The Trustees of the British Museum

### 124. 山水图

元或明
佚名
绢本水墨
手卷
纵25.72、横162.56厘米
明尼阿波利斯美术馆

### River Landscape

Yuan dynasty (1271–1368) or Ming dynasty (1368–1644)
Artist unknown
Ink on silk
Handscroll
H×W : 25.72×162.56 cm
The Minneapolis Institute of Art
Gift of funds from Louis W. Hill, Jr.
Gift of funds from Louis W. Hill, Jr., David Bradford, Myron Kunin, and Bruce Dayton

### 125. 仿范宽山水图     Landscape After Fan Kuan

元或明  Yuan dynasty (1271–1368) or Ming dynasty (1368–1644)
佚名  Artist unknown
绢本设色  Ink and color on silk
册页  Album leaf
纵26.35、横21.59厘米  H×W : 26.35×21.59 cm
洛杉矶郡艺术博物馆  The Los Angeles County Museum of Art
The Phil Berg Collection (M.71.73.120)
© 2024. Digital Image Museum Associates/LACMA/
Art Resource NY/Scala, Florence

### 126. 春山访友图

元
佚名
绢本设色
手卷
纵58.4、横135.9厘米
克利夫兰艺术博物馆

### Visiting Old Friend in Spring Mountains

Yuan dynasty (1271–1368)
Artist unknown
Ink and color on silk
Handscroll
H×W : 58.4×135.9 cm
The Cleveland Museum of Art
Gift of the John Huntington Art and Polytechnic Trust 1919.1021

**127. 雪山行旅图**

元
佚名
绢本设色
册页
纵26.5、横24.6厘米
弗利尔美术馆

**Travelers in Winter Landscape**

Yuan dynasty (1271–1368)
Artist unknown
Ink and color on silk
Album leaf
H×W : 26.5×24.6 cm
The Freer Gallery of Art
Gift of Charles Lang Freer

**128. 峭壁松泉图** **Mountain Torrents**

元或明 Yuan dynasty (1271–1368) or Ming dynasty (1368–1644)
佚名 Artist unknown
绢本水墨 Ink on silk
册页 Album leaf
纵23.1、横24.6厘米 H×W : 23.1×24.6 cm
波士顿艺术博物馆 The Museum of Fine Arts, Boston
Chinese and Japanese Special Fund
© 2024 Museum of Fine Arts, Boston

### 129. 竹林燕居图

元或明
佚名
绢本设色
立轴
纵75.3、横41.9厘米
波士顿艺术博物馆

**Retreat in Bamboo Grove**

Yuan dynasty (1271–1368) or Ming dynasty (1368–1644)
Artist unknown
Ink and color on silk
Hanging scroll
H×W : 75.3×41.9 cm
The Museum of Fine Arts, Boston
Chinese and Japanese Special Fund
© 2024 Museum of Fine Arts, Boston

**130. 柳荫归牧图**

**Herd-boys with Water Buffaloes Under Willow Trees**

元或明
佚名
纸本设色
立轴
纵42.5、横37.3厘米
波士顿艺术博物馆

Yuan dynasty (1271–1368) or Ming dynasty (1368–1644)
Artist unknown
Ink and color on paper
Hanging scroll
H×W : 42.5×37.3 cm
The Museum of Fine Arts, Boston
Chinese and Japanese Special Fund
© 2024 Museum of Fine Arts, Boston

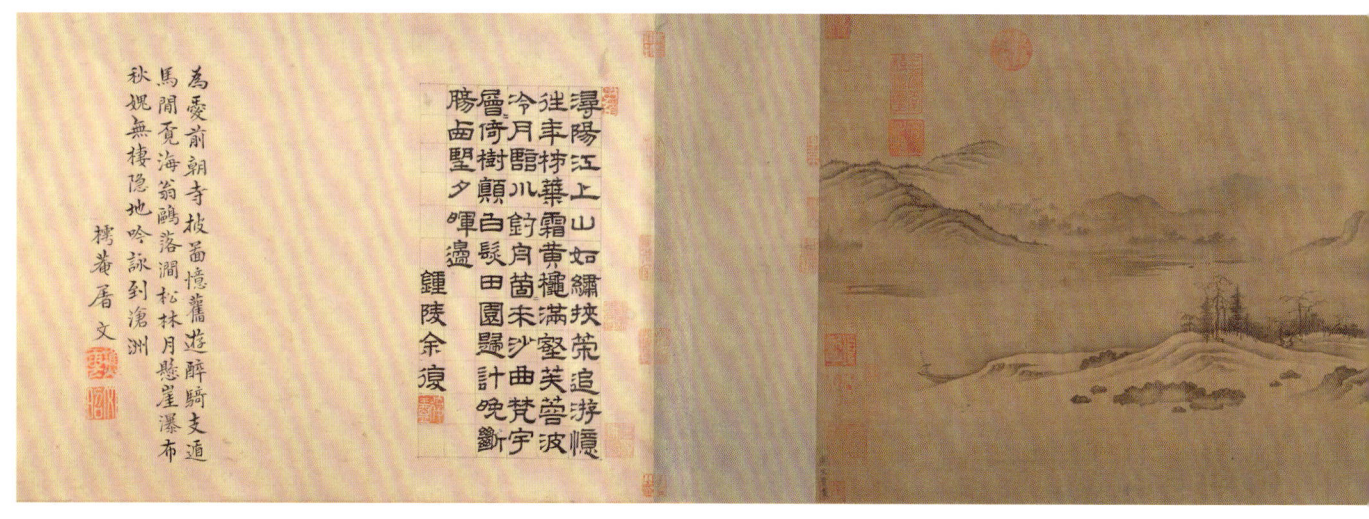

潯陽江上山如繡 挾策追游憶
迤丰抹葉黃橙滿 壑芙蓉波
冷月臨川釣肩菌 朱沙曲梵宇
層倚樹顛白髮田 園題計晚
勝田墅夕暉遍 斷

鍾陵余瓌

為愛前朝寺披圖憶舊遊醉騎支遁
馬閒覓海翁路澗松林月懸崖瀑布
秋煙無棲隱地吟詠到滄洲

樗菴居文

### 131. 秋山萧寺图

元或明
佚名
绢本设色
手卷
纵32.7、横321.3厘米
大都会艺术博物馆

**Buddhist Temples amid Autumn Mountains**

Yuan dynasty (1271–1368) or Ming dynasty (1368–1644)
Artist unknown
Ink and color on silk
Handscroll
H×W : 32.7×321.3 cm
The Metropolitan Museum of Art
Purchase, The Dillon Fund Gift, 1983

野性樂山水澤居遺囊心蕭然紙圍藏後胡跪逢幽居恒
思憶所適縣榘港登臨秋清景無瑕苔翠列逕容霜
餘草孤芳愛雲林崎人集譜俗結宇丹崖陰浮
含不煩遣寄界沖襟況復蕭寺落禪論有遺音算
飄旦自先菩萠如難任挑圖愴兩歷關巖誌巳深景物
匪殊昔但傷箄歎後何當晚度跼歸婦休訕自今

河南高興志題于秀水隱居

秋山望不盡蕭寺貴無雷嚴窣飛霜月樓臺落木風
待船茅店近乘騎野橋通神會燕侯得當時乾與同

前東塔住山 若先

長江浩蕩秋波碧林後行全
沙伭坐中童樹翠模拟美
岩居禹箋千不禱云多梵刹
生遠林二言出逢歸酒乃尔
知晝史真善与一幅生絹傅
至今睒咂生 羅紋

六月閒居塵事寡故人相訪衝門下示我
秋山蕭寺圖云是燕侯之所寫燕侯畫癖
人共知吾心毫素鑒成絲江山楚趙曾編
覽援筆絕境移於斯千巖萬壑氣森然
木落天虛百泉響翠辟含風摩荔懸青
林積雨莓茖長磵谷金銀佛寺閒五雲樓
殿影崔萬聽經繞多羅樹衛法龍逕七
寶臺秋濤江上無天湧浦澈聯蜒野騎
幽人乘暇嘆舟遠客還尋蹯坡龍野騎
寞搜度小橋水遞林下連漁鷟煙岑猿嘯
清襄。蘆洲鷹起輕飄。方知異境不可得
泪沒人閒看遺墨興與鞾舄青我登山
白首歸獨看依佈雲氣上衣襟動我登山
臨水心山中故人偓拾隱結筇擬儔蒼崖陰

長沙蕭規

重文貴與人初師涇京都夏時來
京師市畫款也巳門益上縉神堪苴石素
三洞栴宋志宗帝擅相圖寺機石談搓
中摘丛五而進幀兩上覺其悸芳畫
卯私浸惇俊七夕叙下圍工而亮此狺原
時工有益答李畫院諸达款家某居居六貴
此巻萧寺園心張多士未於但石山房
亭誕誌莧易于宋乖极州群掞卷伕

乙巳二年十月望日睛源叟 陳槐保跋

此卷藏於郎藩竹齋為讓圖端清世下次壬甲戌
夏同午史黃門雲岫出以示余上京孟津今歲二酉云
當見此卷于新安汪景于家今已二十年不知何以至
崇禎八年乙亥七月七日袁樞書時余覿客河北之三年

耶嘗花落過清明春事紀
華江湖兩岸揚州吟沙徑路
山清泠浪過伯生巳有山岭為清明
林江湖伯邀君蔚高齋松香濟呂出不燕又賞秋
山清寺為展拓久囚寓是什何賦起向子上他憶

漫浪越游五十年高嶐龍徹幽雲細眼明仿彿
福中意江峽曾來萬里船
　　　　　天游生陸廣

忽見燕侯畫令人憶舊遊千
巖聞太古萬木簪高秋石路
馳輕驕江風送遠舟人間無此
境舒卷不能住
　　　　　曲江居士錢惟善

己酉歲僞家沈君伯璿家觀燕文貴精妙人神畫
不敢毀辟沈君素藏書卷後勉賦四語後二載復觀
斯卷諸公沛然鑒長編沈君漠素鄙詩故是作
長風吹船過彭蠡縹紗雲夢盡天隙天柱峰迴王
筍造全察夫容半空起岸宗後先多畫師四骸天
機誰以隱燕侯文貴世罕得點染清妍士檀芙斯
崗拂城寶眼前蜂洛石鵑雲
根鐵壁岏徹礴泚尉殿珠樓佛寺中丹墀玉室
仙境柬水邊沙際市橋通野店人家節屋底安期
羨門子拓跋指蓬立面視的吳山塔墀土坏戴漢觀
斯圖慨悒謌謌
　　　　　天游生陸廣

蕭寺大蜜論燕侯名畫揚山橫紅柑他股
領碧雲渦秋床情倘在青骨悉不忘偊
古萵寺園乃燕侯之貴而竹櫻垩武辛
悔芳代事擅緜墙悲御
　　　　　　後伯寺今蕭子燕之大書武寺二
　　　　　　多泊后台乞七囚令車致九家成矣

下與酌清泉步自山南陰蹛掔得出
騰起擔遂後巖依嵌結淨宇面海
廢高扉振衣虛臺迴曾日苦潚
佛鑑畫葵翻經唯老緇竟隔人世靜趣
諮適閱林鳥韋謂非隔人世靜趣
寧多玆久思脫塵網負累勢莫達
遣所遇惆邅想何能卭幽棲射利念
已綠徇名心更遷終尋烟霞侶同赴
滄洲期
八月十三日過顧子羽東溪山隱羽爲
佯證形題蕭寺圖時予勿侵程
擢不淨愚家遂寫題海雲蘭若
詩于其府彭城劉堪識

迴崖列峀樓宇相連嵯峨
楼臺隱隱琤瑽兮噐為已意
秋色渌橋鏗鐘影走夕陽
空雲度楊絳寒雪杳人高
野飯猛猬柏寳子艇舵的
雪逶迤走床襖圖竟
恩佢泗兒
蕭田子勇書

### 132. 秋林鹤逸图 — Landscape with Pavilions and Cranes

元或明  
佚名  
绢本设色  
册页  
纵24.8、横25.4厘米  
大都会艺术博物馆

Yuan dynasty (1271–1368) or Ming dynasty (1368–1644)  
Artist unknown  
Ink and color on silk  
Album leaf  
H×W : 24.8×25.4 cm  
The Metropolitan Museum of Art  
From the Collection of A. W. Bahr, Purchase, Fletcher Fund, 1947

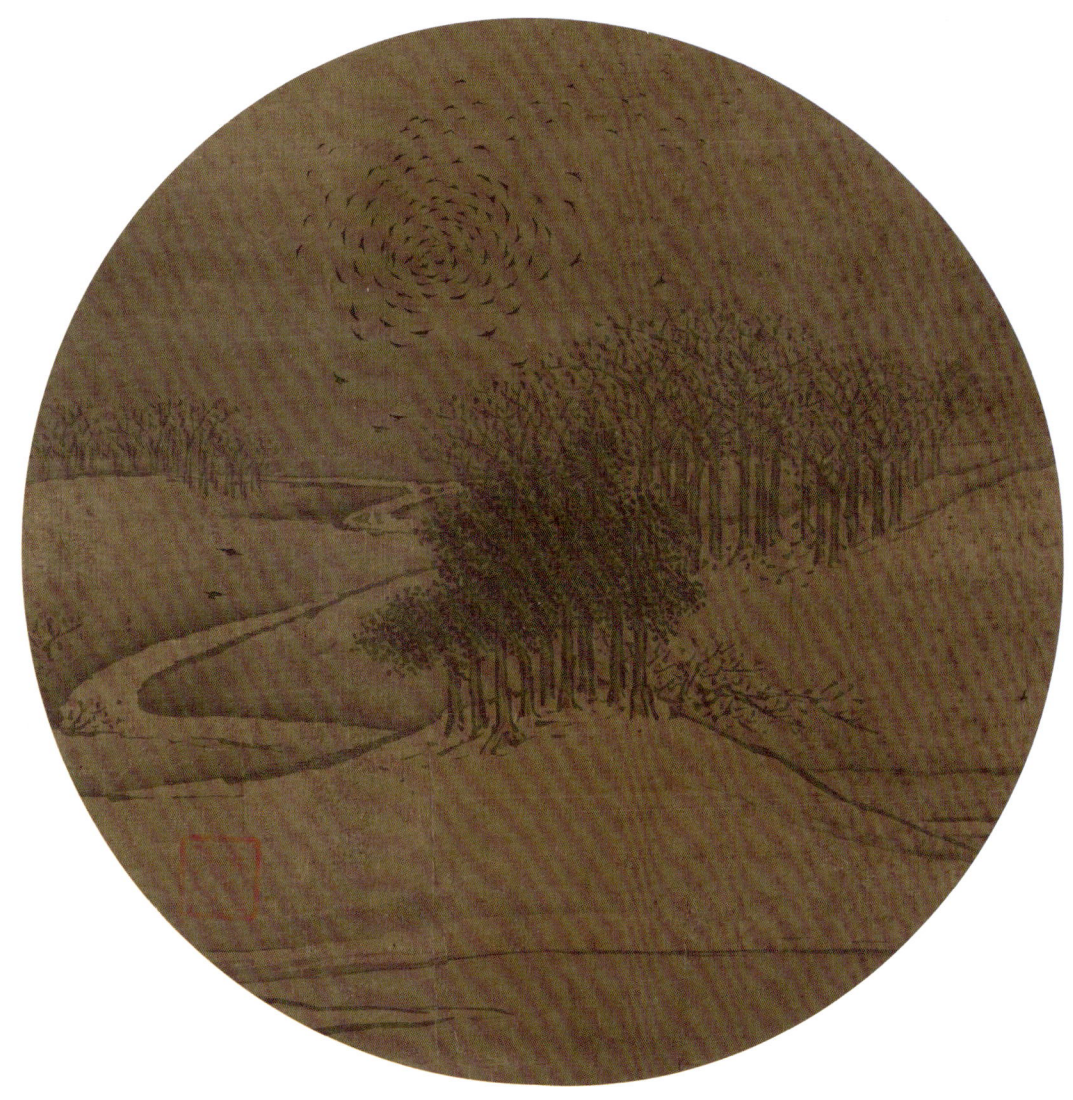

**133. 古木寒鸦图**

元
佚名
绢本设色
册页
纵41.6、横37.3厘米
大都会艺术博物馆

**Crows and Bare Trees in Winter**

Yuan dynasty (1271–1368)
Artist unknown
Ink and color on silk
Album leaf
H×W : 41.6×37.3 cm
The Metropolitan Museum of Art
Purchase, The Dillon Fund Gift, 1982

**134. 秋艳图**

元或明
佚名
绢本设色
册页
纵20.3、横20.6厘米
大都会艺术博物馆

**Autumn Splendor**

Yuan dynasty (1271–1368) or Ming dynasty (1368–1644)
Artist unknown
Ink and color on silk
Album leaf
H×W : 20.3×20.6 cm
The Metropolitan Museum of Art
John Stewart Kennedy Fund, 1913

### 135. 牡丹图

**Peonies**

| | |
|---|---|
| 元或明 | Yuan dynasty (1271–1368) or Ming dynasty (1368–1644) |
| 佚名 | Artist unknown |
| 绢本设色 | Ink and color on silk |
| 立轴 | Hanging scroll |
| 纵145.5、横88.3厘米 | H×W : 145.5×88.3 cm |
| 克利夫兰艺术博物馆 | The Cleveland Museum of Art |
| | John L. Severance Fund 1976.90 |

**136. 虫草花卉图**

元
佚名
绢本设色
册页
纵22.4、横23.2厘米
耶鲁大学艺术博物馆

**Melon Flowers and Insects**

Yuan dynasty (1271–1368)
Artist unknown
Ink and color on silk
Album leaf
H×W : 22.4×23.2 cm
The Yale University Art Gallery
Mary Griggs Burke Collection, Gift of the Mary and Jackson Burke Foundation

**137. 莲花图**

元或明
佚名
绢本设色
立轴
纵141.6、横67.9厘米
大都会艺术博物馆

**Lotus and Waterbirds**

Yuan dynasty (1271–1368) or Ming dynasty (1368–1644)
Artist unknown
Ink and color on silk
Hanging scrolls
H×W : 141.6×67.9 cm
The Metropolitan Museum of Art
Purchase, The Dillon Fund Gift, 1988

**138. 粉白荷花图**

元或明
佚名
绢本设色
立轴
纵136、横60.7厘米
金贝尔艺术博物馆

**Pink and White Lotus**

Yuan dynasty (1271–1368) or Ming dynasty (1368–1644)
Artist unknown
Ink and color on silk
Hanging scroll
H×W : 136×60.7 cm
The Kimbell Art Museum
Kimbell Art Museum, Fort Worth, Texas.
AP 1984.19

### 139. 花鸟图

| | |
|---|---|
| 元或明 | Yuan dynasty (1271–1368) or Ming dynasty (1368–1644) |
| 佚名 | Artist unknown |
| 纸本设色 | Ink and color on paper |
| 册页 | Album leaf |
| 纵29.4、横28.8厘米 | H×W : 29.4×28.8 cm |
| 克利夫兰艺术博物馆 | The Cleveland Museum of Art |
| | John L. Severance Fund 1970.70 |

**Flowers and Birds**

**140. 长臂猿图**

金
佚名
绢本水墨
册页
纵24.4、横23.8厘米
大都会艺术博物馆

**Gibbon Seated on Branch**

Jin dynasty (1115–1234)
Artist unknown
Ink on silk
Album leaf
H×W : 24.4×23.8 cm
The Metropolitan Museum of Art
John Stewart Kennedy Fund, 1913

**141. 猿猴图**

元
佚名
纸本水墨
册页
直径：22.9厘米
克利夫兰艺术博物馆

**Monkey**

Yuan dynasty (1271–1368)
Artist unknown
Ink on paper
Album leaf
Diameter: 22.9 cm
The Cleveland Museum of Art
Gift of the John Huntington Art and
Polytechnic Trust 1915.620

**142. 猛禽图**

元或明
佚名
绢本设色
册页
纵32.6、横26.2厘米
弗利尔美术馆

**Hawk on Leafless Branch**

Yuan dynasty (1271–1368) or Ming dynasty (1368–1644)
Artist unknown
Ink and color on silk
Album leaf
H×W : 32.6×26.2 cm
The Freer Gallery of Art
Gift of Charles Lang Freer

**143. 猎犬图**

元或明
佚名
绢本设色
册页
纵28.4、横27.1厘米
波士顿艺术博物馆

**Hound Walking**

Yuan dynasty (1271–1368) or Ming dynasty (1368–1644)
Artist unknown
Ink and color on silk
Album leaf
H×W : 28.4×27.1 cm
The Museum of Fine Arts, Boston
William Sturgis Bigelow Collection
© 2024 Museum of Fine Arts, Boston

**144. 龙虎图之虎**

元
佚名
绢本水墨
立轴
纵80.5、横40.3厘米
大都会艺术博物馆

**Tiger**

Yuan dynasty (1271–1368)
Artist unknown
Ink on silk
Hanging scroll
H×W : 80.5×40.3 cm
The Metropolitan Museum of Art
Gift of Mr. and Mrs. Kwan S. Wong, 1986

## 145. 龙虎图之龙 — Dragon

元  
佚名  
绢本水墨  
立轴  
纵80.5、横40.3厘米  
大都会艺术博物馆

Yuan dynasty (1271–1368)  
Artist unknown  
Ink on silk  
Hanging scroll  
H×W : 80.5×40.3 cm  
The Metropolitan Museum of Art  
Gift of Mr. and Mrs. Kwan S. Wong, 1987

### 146. 鱼藻图

元或明
佚名
绢本水墨
立轴
纵89.6、横48.3厘米
波士顿艺术博物馆

### Fish Among Water Plants

Yuan dynasty (1271–1368) or Ming dynasty (1368–1644)
Artist unknown
Ink on silk
Hanging scroll
H×W: 89.6×48.3 cm
The Museum of Fine Arts, Boston
William Sturgis Bigelow Collection
© 2024 Museum of Fine Arts, Boston

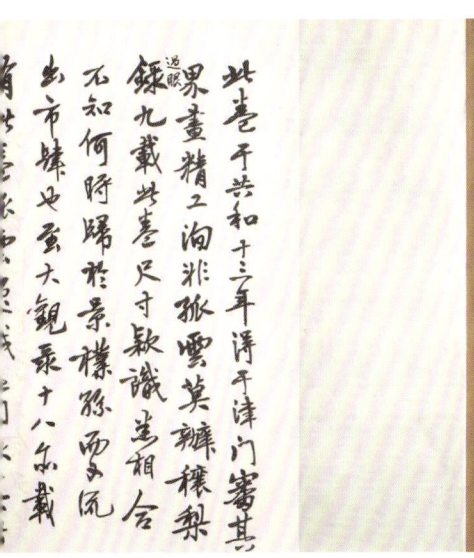
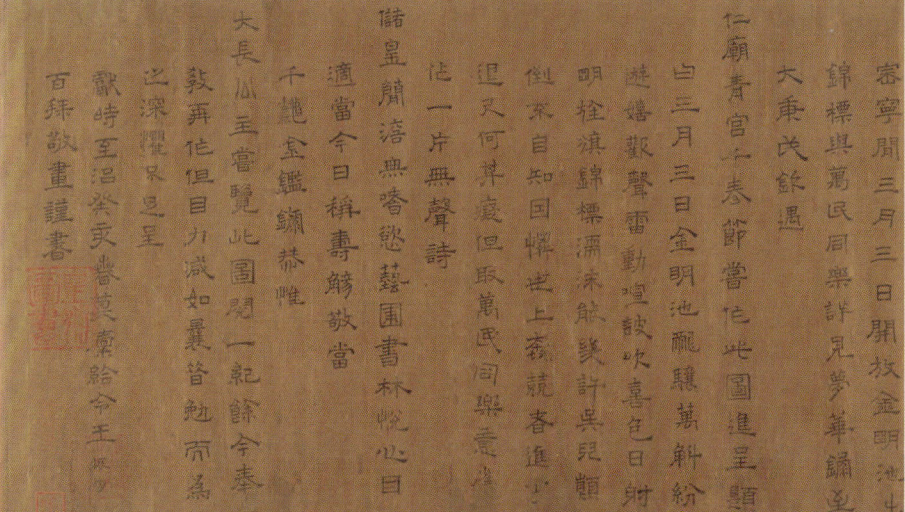

### 147. 金明池争標图

元
佚名
绢本水墨
手卷
尺寸不详
大都会艺术博物馆

**Dragon Boat Regatta on Jinming Lake**

Yuan dynasty (1271–1368)
Artist unknown
Ink on silk
Handscroll
Dimensions unknown
The Metropolitan Museum of Art
Purchase, Bequest of Dorothy Graham Bennett, 1966

### 148. 墨龙图

元或明
佚名
纸本水墨
手卷
纵44.8、横190.8厘米
大都会艺术博物馆

### Dragons and Landscape

Yuan dynasty (1271–1368) or Ming dynasty (1368–1644)
Artist unknown
Ink on paper
Handscroll
H×W : 44.8×190.8 cm
The Metropolitan Museum of Art
H. O. Havemeyer Collection, Bequest of Mrs. H. O. Havemeyer, 1929

### 149. 雪山行旅图

元或明
佚名
绢本水墨
册页
纵25.1、横25.9厘米
弗利尔美术馆

**Mule-train in Snowy Mountains**

Yuan dynasty (1271–1368) or Ming dynasty (1368–1644)
Artist unknown
Ink on silk
Album leaf
H×W : 25.1×25.9 cm
The Freer Gallery of Art
Gift of Charles Lang Freer

**150. 古木竹禽图**     **Old Tree Bamboo and Birds**

元或明  
佚名  
绢本设色  
册页  
纵25.2、横25.7厘米  
大都会艺术博物馆

Yuan dynasty (1271–1368) or Ming dynasty (1368–1644)  
Aritist unknown  
Ink and color on silk  
Album leaf  
H×W : 25.2×25.7 cm  
The Metropolitan Museum of Art  
From the Collection of A. W. Bahr, Purchase, Fletcher Fund, 1947

# 版权支持

（按中文馆名音序排列）

鲍尔基金会鲍氏东方艺术馆
贝纳基博物馆
波士顿艺术博物馆
不列颠博物馆
大阪市立东洋陶瓷美术馆
大阪市立美术馆
大都会艺术博物馆
东京国立博物馆
费城艺术博物馆
菲尔德博物馆
弗利尔美术馆
弗利尔与赛克勒美术馆
哈佛艺术博物馆
荷兰国立博物馆
集美博物馆
金贝尔艺术博物馆
凯布朗利博物馆
克利夫兰艺术博物馆
科隆东亚艺术博物馆
洛杉矶郡艺术博物馆
明尼阿波利斯美术馆
奈良国立博物馆
普林斯顿大学美术馆
赛克勒博物馆
赛克勒美术馆
圣路易斯艺术博物馆
维多利亚和阿尔伯特博物馆
新南威尔士州美术馆
辛辛那提艺术博物馆
亚洲文明博物馆
耶鲁大学艺术博物馆
印第安纳波利斯艺术博物馆
芝加哥艺术博物馆

# Image Contributors

(In Chinese Pinyin Order)

The Baur Foundation, Museum of Far Eastern Art
The Benaki Museum
The Museum of Fine Arts, Boston
The British Museum
The Museum of Oriental Ceramics, Osaka
The Osaka City Museum of Fine Arts
The Metropolitan Museum of Art
The Tokyo National Museum
The Philadelphia Museum of Art
The Field Museum
The Freer Gallery of Art
The Freer and the Arthur M. Sackler Gallery
The Harvard Art Museums
The Rijksmuseum
The Guimet Museum
The Kimbell Art Museum
The Quai Branly Museum
The Cleveland Museum of Art
The Museum of East Asian Art, Cologne
The Los Angeles County Museum of Art
The Minneapolis Institute of Art
The Nara National Museum
The Princeton University Art Museum
The Arthur M. Sackler Museum
The Arthur M. Sackler Gallery
The Saint Louis Art Museum
The Victoria and Albert Museum
The Art Gallery of New South Wales
The Cincinnati Art Museum
The Asian Civilisations Museum
The Yale University Art Gallery
The Indianapolis Museum of Art
The Art Institute of Chicago

# 编辑、出版人员

总 策 划　马汝军　谢　刚
选题策划　孙志鹏
主任编辑　邹懿男
出版统筹　丁　宁

责任编辑　李文彧　林　琳
特约编辑　丁文文
编　　辑　陈　雯　张小君　汪　欣　孙立英　白华召　施　然　马　源
　　　　　赵笑笑　刘　琦　黄　艳　王　萌　王颖洁　王宏亮　毕力格图
责任校对　刘　义
实习编辑　齐倩颖　潘泓瑾

英文翻译　丁文文　耿玮浩
英文审校　韩　华

装帧设计　冷暖儿
图文版式　魏　丹　杨　丹　阮鸽鸽
责任印制　韦　舰　李珊珊

# Editorial Staff

**Chief Publisher**　Ma Rujun　Xie Gang

**Publisher**　Sun Zhipeng

**Editorial Director**　Zou Yinan

**Publishing Coordinator**　Ding Ning

**Editors-in-Charge**　Li Wenyu　Lin Lin

**Contributing Editor**　Ding Wenwen

**Editors**　Chen Wen　Zhang Xiaojun　Wang Xin　Sun Liying　Bai Huazhao　Shi Ran　Ma Yuan　　Zhao Xiaoxiao　Liu Qi　Huang Yan　Wang Meng　Wang Yingjie　Wang Hongliang　Biligt

**Responsible Proofreader**　Liu Yi

**Interns**　Qi Qianying　Pan Hongjin

**English Translators**　Ding Wenwen　Geng Weihao

**English Proofreader**　Han Hua

**Cover Designer**　Leng Nuaner

**Layout Designers**　Wei Dan　Yang Dan　Ruan Gege

**Responsible Printing Coordinators**　Wei Jian　Li Shanshan